U.S. Healthcare
on Life Support

U.S. Healthcare on Life Support

RESUSCITATING THE DYING SYSTEM

Stephen E. Weinberg, MD FACC

Foreword by Lawton R. Burns, PhD, MBA

Denisher Press
HADDONFIELD, NJ

Although the author and publisher have made every effort to ensure the accuracy and completeness of information contained in this book, we assume no responsibility for errors, inaccuracies, omissions, or any inconsistency herein. Any slighting of people, places, or organizations is unintentional.

First printing 2007
ISBN 978-0-9793802-3-5
LCCN 2007922860

ATTENTION CORPORATIONS, UNIVERSITIES, COLLEGES, AND PROFESSIONAL ORGANIZATIONS: Quantity discounts are available on bulk purchases of this book for educational or gift purposes or as premiums for increasing magazine subscriptions or renewals. Special books or book excerpts can also be created to fit specific needs. For information, please contact Denisher Press, PO Box 71, Haddonfield, NJ 08033-9998; ph 856-795-0775; fax 856-795-6109.

DEDICATION

This book is dedicated to my patients who have suffered with serious illnesses and to many of them who have had to suffer the additional insult of having poor health insurance, often causing them to choose between food and medications. My hope is that this exposé will inspire a comprehensive, nationwide discussion regarding the inequities of healthcare financing that will ultimately allow my patients to receive truly affordable healthcare.

ACKNOWLEDGMENTS

For nearly four decades, my wife Denise has endured late dinners, interrupted plans, and being awakened nights and weekends when I am on call. She offered sage advice to me when I was managing partner of our group practice. While I wrote this book, she was my harshest editor, and her input is felt on virtually every page.

Despite my not always being there for them because of practice obligations, my children, Nicole and Sheryl, have never complained and have always been loving and supportive of my efforts. This has made the time away from them easier. Brian has always been enthusiastic, supportive, and continuously helpful with my technology needs.

One of my partners, Richard Dickstein, MD, has always been there since I was an intern nearly forty years ago. He has provided me with guidance and criticism during the development of this manuscript.

The manuscript would not have come together without the expert editorial assistance from Allan Burns, for which I am very grateful.

TABLE OF CONTENTS

FOREWORD

During my thirty years of study, I have read many books written by physicians about the U.S. healthcare system. Most of these books describe how physicians are trained, what the major rites of passage are, what crises they face in their hospitals and practices, and how the profession of medicine is changing.

Dr. Weinberg's book takes a different path. Steve has spent considerable time analyzing the microeconomics and macroeconomics of the industry in which physicians practice. He details very clearly how the practice of medicine intersects (and sometimes collides with) the world of rising unit costs, the increasingly constrained reimbursement environment, and the incessant push for cost containment. He has packaged it all here in a very tidy fashion that is easily consumed by both practitioners and non-practitioners alike.

Where Steve got all the time to write this book, I do not know. I have known Steve professionally for over a decade and am only too familiar with the lengthy hours he and his colleagues put in weekly on a routine basis—whether seeing patients, running a large group practice in cardiology, or traveling across the Delaware River from New Jersey into Philadelphia to teach Wharton School students what it is like to be a practicing specialist in a tough insurance market. I can only give a lot of credit to a generation of well-trained specialists like Steve who work hard, have a passion for what they do, and persist in their profession—despite the mounting challenges and frustrations they face.

What I do know is that Steve's lengthy tenure as both a cardiologist (nearly thirty years) and group practice managing partner (twelve years) enables him to view the industry and the practice of medicine in a unique fashion. Steve combines the big picture view of a macroeconomist with the intimate knowledge of a hands-on practitioner. His analysis moves easily back and forth between these two perspectives. The result is an integrated, balanced presentation. In a good sense, he is bipolar.

This book gives non-physicians a view of the healthcare industry from the learned perspective of a key professional actor at the center of our healthcare system: the physician. It is a poignant view. For example, few lay people really understand the trajectory of health episodes and attendant costs of patients that delay seeking treatment for heart conditions, which Steve outlines on the first page of the Introduction. Few people understand the importance of pricing in healthcare, which Steve explores in Chapter 1. And few lay people really understand all of the time physicians devote to treating and talking to patients, time and effort that is often not reimbursed (a topic Steve addresses in Chapter 2).

There is a certain irony in Steve's exposition. Physicians technically have a monopoly over most of the key decisions in healthcare. They control who gets a prescription for a drug; they control who gets admitted to a hospital; they control who gets access to specialized equipment and procedures. And, yet, despite this monopoly, physicians are caught in between powerful economic and societal forces and other powerful actors that constrain what they are able to accomplish. Both of these facts are central to Steve's analysis, which is another facet of the balanced view offered by the book.

Like Steve, I believe that people who seek to reform our healthcare system need to understand how it operates at the local level—such as the daily delivery of patient care by physicians. They will need to be able to relate the impact of reforms at the macroeconomic level to the local practice of medicine and delivery of care. This book helps to inculcate this understanding. I think we can all learn a lot from our physicians—not just about how to take better care of ourselves, but also how to take better care of our healthcare system.

—**Lawton R. Burns, PhD, MBA,** *James Joo-Jin Kim Professor,*
Director, Wharton Center for Health Management and Economics,
The Wharton School, University of Pennsylvania

INTRODUCTION

It was 10 P.M. when an ambulance rolled into a local emergency room. In the ambulance was Roger, a forty-five-year-old factory worker, husband, and father of two children ages ten and thirteen. His wife had called 911 because he had been complaining of chest pain for about eighteen hours. His father had a history of heart disease, diagnosed at age fifty. Though Roger was concerned that he might be having a heart attack, he still thought that it could just be indigestion and did not want to come to the hospital for fear that he would have to stay overnight. Roger had health insurance through his employment, but the deductible for a hospitalization was $350, and his copayment was 15% of the total bill, which he did not have. When the diagnosis of a large heart attack was made within minutes of his arrival, Roger was immediately taken to the catheterization laboratory by one of my partners, and the blockage in his heart artery was opened using a balloon and a stent.

Over the next two days, tests indicated major heart damage that was likely permanent because of his delay in coming to the hospital. He was diagnosed as having heart failure as a result of the large heart attack and was finally discharged from the hospital six days later. He was prescribed numerous medications and was asked to see me, a cardiologist, in two weeks. Roger did not have prescription drug insurance, so the medications cost about $400 for the first month and each month thereafter. I saw Roger several times in the office over the next year. As predicted, the damage to his heart was very extensive and permanent. He required the insertion of a defibrillator to protect him from sudden death as a result of an unstable heart rhythm.

He was unable to return to work because of the demanding physical aspects of his job. The company was "unable" to find a suitable job for

Roger, so he was fired. He has tried to find other employment but has been unsuccessful. His wife has gone back to work as a secretary, making about $12 an hour with minimal health benefits. It costs her about $450 per month to purchase health insurance for Roger, with high deductibles and no drug benefits. For financial reasons, Roger can only purchase about one-half of his medications. He comes to see me periodically for cardiac care but has a copayment of $35 for each visit, making it difficult for him to keep all of his appointments. He cannot afford to have an EKG, stress test, or blood work as a result of insufficient coverage and the high copayments. I give him samples of his medications whenever I can and often do not charge him for tests that I can do in the office. He is anxious to go back to work, but it is difficult to find a job that is appropriate for his skills and his medical condition. He is going back to school to try to learn a new trade. Roger is unable to play sports with his children and to enjoy a full lifestyle in view of his physical disability. His long-term prognosis and life expectancy are only fair as a result of the size of the heart attack. His savings, what little there was, are gone, and he is at his wits' end. He worked hard all his life and provided for his family the best he could.

Roger is facing a substantially shorter life span than normal. It will be filled with hospitalizations, frequent medical testing, consumption of numerous medications daily, great expense, and anxiety. His wife and children will likely be deprived of his ability to earn a reasonable income and the enjoyment of having Roger with them for many years. He may end up on Medicaid, if he qualifies, or perhaps Social Security disability, at which point we will all be paying for his long-term care—which will be very expensive. His life is ruined because he delayed coming to the hospital when he first experienced chest pain. He was most concerned about his inability to pay the $350 deductible and his hospital copayment!

This is not an unusual story. Many physicians encounter similar situations daily in all specialties of medicine: the fifty-year-old woman with a large breast mass that turns out to be advanced cancer; the sixty-year-old man with rectal bleeding who has cancer of the bowel; the forty-five-year-old man who has an infection on his leg due to a relatively minor injury that now has spiraled into bacteria in his blood and low blood pressure from an overwhelming infection. Many times these patients do not come to the doctor because of fear of the expense. Other very serious problems arise as a result of patients being unable to afford their medications; therefore, they take them less frequently to make them last longer. Patients often do not come for scheduled visits or preventive care as a result of the expense. These visits could detect illnesses before they become serious and life threatening. Later detection results in more complicated treatment, which is more expensive and has a smaller chance of success.

With forty-eight million people uninsured, fifty-one million people on Medicaid, and at least sixteen million people (probably more) underinsured, more than one-third of the United States population is without adequate health insurance. *The United States is the only industrialized country in the world that does not mandate quality health insurance for all of its citizens!*

Many books, journals, newspaper articles, and televised documentaries have been written and produced discussing the healthcare crisis in this country from the standpoint of quality, cost, access, and comparisons with other industrialized countries of the world. Usually, these discussions focus on isolated aspects of the healthcare system, such as insurance companies, hospitals, pharmaceutical companies, physicians, the indigent or uninsured. We have all heard the statistics of how the United States has the most costly system by far, with forty-eight million people uninsured, high infant mortality rates, decreasing access to care, quality of care issues, long waits in emergency rooms, insurance premiums escalating faster than the cost of living, and many other concerns. Few, if any of us, believe our system is fair, affordable, compassionate to the indigent, worth the costs, and as safe as it should be. Most of us feel the healthcare industry is on "life support" and about to take its last dying breath. It seems that everyone knows someone like Roger or has an anecdote about some negative aspect of our healthcare system. They are only too glad to share their stories when prompted. Many of these stories contain valid criticisms, but we need to gain an in-depth understanding of the system and how it really works in order to achieve a more accurate view of the problems we confront. Only then can we decide how to fix the system without further injuring a relatively fragile healthcare industry or destroying it altogether.

Since beginning medical school in 1967, I have seen incredible changes in all fields of medicine, but I have extensive firsthand knowledge of the innovations in cardiology. Coronary bypass surgery, angioplasty, stents, pacemakers, revolutionary drugs, and more have extended a high quality of life to tens of millions of people. As a practicing cardiologist for almost thirty years and the managing partner of a twenty-two person cardiology group for twelve years, I have seen dramatic changes in the business of medicine as well and have been directly involved with organized medicine, insurance companies, hospital finance and strategic planning, malpractice insurance financing, and the day-to-day running of a busy practice.

Most people who have written about the healthcare financing subject have been economists, reporters, government employees, policy makers, and think tank representatives. They have gone about the task of trying to define the problem by conducting interviews and pouring through tons of statistics. They have not lived the problem for thirty-five years as I have.

This discussion will not be a bleeding-heart (no pun intended) enumeration of the virtues of physicians and the healthcare system, but rather a well-annotated, detailed look at the healthcare "industry". However, I feel strongly that medicine *is* a noble profession, and it is very painful for me to see the system functioning poorly, not providing high-quality care to all Americans, and costing so much that people often must choose between food and healthcare.

In order for policy makers, legislators, and, yes, us, the American people, to fix the system of healthcare financing and improve the quality and efficiency, we must first understand it completely and be willing to engage in a national debate regarding what we want.

The purpose of this book is to provide information so that readers can clearly understand the healthcare financing system in the United States and participate in the debate. Having been in discussions with lawmakers and numerous consultants over many years, I am convinced that many of them lack a deep understanding of large pieces of the problem, and some have little knowledge of any part of the entire problem. This is the only concise and comprehensive book discussing all the relevant issues. I will try to be objective and annotate the information when possible and provide real-life examples of issues confronted by me and my practice. Since our system is often compared to other industrialized countries, in particular Canada, I will explore the similarities and differences when they are relevant.

If you lack a comprehensive understanding of the issues and do not take part in what should be a national discussion, you will lose the opportunity to express your desires as to how you want your healthcare system to function and how it will be financed. Your personal health, longevity, and quality of life are at stake, as well as your money. The system is on life support and is in danger of not surviving, and, if it fails, we will all pay the price.

CHAPTER 1

The Problem: Economics 101

This chapter will explore the costs of healthcare in the United States and other industrialized countries, in particular Canada. To determine why we spend more per capita than other countries, I will analyze the costs of personnel, drugs, and administering the entire system, which together constitute the vast majority of expenses of the United States and Canada. One theory is that we utilize more services and drugs per capita than Canada and other industrialized countries. I believe this is not the case and that the most important differential is pricing, both for physicians and non-physician professionals, as well as the unit pricing for drugs. I will show that physician fees for service and the hourly wage for non-physician professionals are much higher in the United States. The other huge factor is the cost of administering our complex system compared to the single payer system in Canada and most other countries.

In order to understand and compare the relative costs of healthcare in various countries so that we can clearly see the problem facing the U.S., it is imperative that we define the terminology we will use and delineate the cross-country comparisons.

When we speak of international comparisons, we are usually talking about information generated within the Organization for Economic Co-operation and Development (OECD), which is a thirty-member consortium of industrialized nations that share information on many aspects of their societies, one of which is healthcare data. This entity includes the United States, Japan, Canada, France, the United Kingdom, and other countries primarily in Europe. The last complete OECD report, published in 2005 and based on 2003 information, revealed the total U.S. healthcare per capita (per person) expenditure to be $5,635. The average for all thirty countries was $2,306. The U.S. expenditure was about 2.4 times the average of all the countries.[1] The numbers represented are in what is called "Purchasing Power Parities" (PPP), which is based upon a formula that attempts to equilibrate each country's standard of living and thereby equalize its citizens' purchasing power so comparisons can be made. The reference currency is the U.S. dollar.

To look at the cost differentials in a slightly different way: We are spending about $3,300 per person per year more on healthcare than the average industrialized OECD country and about $1,800 more than the next highest country, Norway. In any event, the amount of money spent on healthcare in the U.S. is huge in comparison to other industrialized countries, and therein lies the problem we are confronting. It is as simple as that!

The real issues are: Why are our costs so high? Can we do anything within reason to reduce them? And are we getting our money's worth?

The cost of healthcare is the product of the cost of a unit of care times the number of units (cost/unit x # of units). For example, the cost of caring for an outpatient of mine during a year would be the number of office visits multiplied by the cost of each visit, the number of tests multiplied by the cost of each test, and the number of drugs multiplied by the cost of each drug. Data from the OECD indicates that the number of physician visits, hospital days, and admissions per year per capita is less in the U.S. than the median for all thirty countries.[2] *Therefore, if the number of encounters or units of care is less than most of the other industrialized countries, it must be the prices per unit that are the driving force behind our huge cost differences.* These findings that apply to the OECD, in general, also apply to Canada and, in some instances, the reduced utilization in the U.S. is striking.[3]

In an effort to analyze our costs more closely and to draw reasonable conclusions, I will compare our healthcare system expenses to those in Canada. I have chosen Canada because we are in close proximity, speak the same language (or nearly so), and have both open borders and much in common. I will take each element of the healthcare expenditure and calculate the excess cost in the U.S. based solely upon the differential created by increased expense for salaries, unit drug pricing, and administration. Later in the book, I will take each of these differentials and discuss them in further detail.

The Canadian System

In column 1, I have listed the breakdown of Canadian expenses as documented by the Canadian Institute for Health Information in 2003. In column 2, these values are converted into U.S. dollars Purchasing Power Parity (PPP), and the analysis will use the conversion throughout. Column 3 demonstrates the Canadian expenses per capita. Column 4 shows the increases the Canadian system would face if it had to "play by American rules". The discussion of this continues below.[4, 5]

	1 Canadian expenses in $Canadian in billions	2 Canadian expenses in $U.S. PPP in billions	3 Canadian expenses per person in $U.S. PPP	4 Increased expenses in $U.S. PPP billions	5 New Total Canadian expense $U.S. PPP in billions	6 Increased expenses per person (Canada) $U.S. PPP	7 New Total Canadian expense per person $U.S. PPP
Hospitals	37.2	30.0	949	19.5	49.5	617	1566
Drugs	20.1	16.2	513	11.0	27.2	348	861
Physicians	16.1	13.0	411	4.7	17.7	148	559
Other professionals	13.2	10.6	337	3.8	14.5	121	458
Other institutions	11.4	9.2	291	6.0	15.2	189	480
Capital	5.6	4.5	143		4.5		143
Administration	4.9	4.0	125	41.0	45.0	1,298	1423
Public health	6.9	5.6	176	3.5	9.0	109	285
Other spending	7.4	6.0	189		6.0		189
Total	122.8	99.0	3,134		188.5	2,831	5965

Physician Salaries

A salary survey from 2002 noted that U.S. physicians on average earned about 1.5 times the amount of Canadian physicians after expenses ($179,000 vs. $117,000).[6] Part of the explanation for the higher salaries is that, in many instances, the U.S. fees for service in U.S. dollars PPP are about twice those in Canada for similar procedures. Therefore, if Canada had to incur a similar relative cost of U.S. physician salaries, the additional cost of physician expenditures in Canada would be about $4.7 billion or a total expense of $17.7 billion. Whether this additional expense is reasonable is the subject of a later chapter. For now, we will just keep track of this number.

Drug Costs

The cost of prescription drugs is a significant part of the total healthcare expenditure, amounting to about 16% of the total budget or $20 billion in Canadian currency.[7] It is estimated that the per unit Canadian drug costs are about 60% of those of the U.S.[8, 9] In other words, on average the cost per pill or dose of injectable medication is significantly lower in Canada compared to the U.S., corrected for PPP. This is already known by many Americans who are purchasing numerous drugs from Canada as a result of the lower prices. It is also estimated that the number of units of consumption per capita is similar in both countries.[10] Therefore, the additional expense in the U.S. attributed to drugs would be the costs per unit. According to this analysis, if Canada had drug pricing similar to the U.S., the additional cost in Canada would be about $11 billion, and the total cost would be about $27 billion. Again, hold on to these numbers, as we will discuss pharmaceutical issues in another chapter.

Hospital Analysis

In 2003 the U.S. spent about $515 billion or 31% of its healthcare budget on hospital care. The cost of hospital care in Canada was about $37 billion or 30% of the total healthcare expenditure.[11] Canadian hospital expenses are made up of non-physician salaries and benefits (68%), drugs (3%), medical supplies (19%), physician costs (4%), and other miscellaneous items (6%).[12] The average hourly salary for non-physician hospital workers in the United States was about $25 and in Canada about $14.75.[13, 14, 15] The ratio is about 1.7, quite similar to the physician salary ratio. Using the same analysis as above for salaries and drugs (multiplying physician salaries by 1.5, non-physician salaries by 1.7, and drugs by 1.6), the excess cost of hospital services in Canada would be about $19.5 billion with a total cost of $50 billion if Canada had to absorb the excess costs of the U.S. Hold on to these numbers as well.

Administration Costs

The cost of administering the entire healthcare system in the U.S. has been discussed as being a source of huge excess expense as compared to other countries that have a "single-payer" system, as most do, including Canada. A single-payer system is one in which all, or virtually all, of the citizens of a particular country fall under one organization to which premiums are paid and from which disbursements are made. The administrative expenses are defined as insurance company overhead (including profits of private insurance companies), employers' costs to manage health benefits, brokerage commissions, consultants fees, hospital and nursing home administration, administrative costs of practitioners, home care, and Medicare/Medicaid overhead. A landmark Harvard study by Woolhandler, et al. estimated that the cost of administering the entire healthcare system in Canada was about 16.7% of the total expenditure and in the U.S. about 31%. The excess cost to administer the U.S. healthcare system compared to Canada in 1999, using $U.S. PPP, was about $752 per person. If we apply the same percentages to the 2003 expenditures, the cost in Canada was $524 vs. $1,822 per person in the U.S. for a difference of $1,298.[16] It is likely that the difference in 2003, the year under consideration, was even higher in view of the fact that private insurance companies in the U.S. have been making extremely high profits in recent years. Additional discussions about administering the healthcare system will also be undertaken in later chapters.

Column 5 above is the "new total expense" Canada would incur if it had the same salary scale, per unit drug costs, and administrative expenses as the U.S. (or column 2 plus 4). Column 6 is the increased costs per person. Column 7 is the "new" costs expressed per person. The largest additional expense by far was the cost of administrating the system, which was, as stated above, about $1,298 per person.

So What Do All These Numbers Really Mean?

The U.S. spent about $5,635 per person on healthcare in 2003 and, remarkably, Canada would have spent $5,965 per person if it had the same relative costs as the U.S. for salaries, drugs/devices, and administration. Since these numbers are normalized by pricing per unit, one could argue that the slightly lower expenditure in the U.S. may be a result of fewer resources utilized and a more efficient system except for the administration piece.

The issues of concern are: Why are the costs of salaries, drugs, and administration so high in the U.S. compared to Canada, and what can be done, if anything, to bring them in line with other countries? That, as the saying goes, is the $64,000 (or more appropriately the multi-billion dollar) question!!

The next several chapters will look at each of these categories of expense and analyze them completely to see if they are "reasonable" and what can be done to bring them down or at least keep them from increasing rapidly.

CHAPTER 2

The People Cost

This chapter will focus on the costs incurred by the healthcare system for payments to physicians and for the salaries of other healthcare professionals. As we saw in Chapter 1, U.S. physician income is significantly higher (1.5 times) than in Canada. Furthermore, median physician income in the U.S. was about 2.8 times the median income of the other OECD physicians in a 1996 survey (the last time such a survey was conducted).[1] Is there a reasonable explanation for these relatively higher physician salaries in the U.S.?

The Wage Disparities

The overall salary structure in the U.S. is probably one of the most important reasons the cost of healthcare is so high compared to other countries. In a research article, Uwe Reinhardt, a renowned healthcare economist from Princeton University, states:

> the incomes of highly skilled health care workers—notably physicians—are determined partly with reference to the incomes that equally able and skilled professionals can earn elsewhere in the economy. Because the U.S. distribution of earned income for all occupations is wider than it is in most other OECD countries, the relatively high incomes offered skilled professionals in the United States may well have

served to pull up the incomes of American physicians relative to the incomes of their peers abroad.[2]

In other words, the difference between the average highest incomes and
the average lowest incomes in the U.S. is greater than in most other industrialized countries and is increasing annually.

One could argue that this is at least partly a result of more socialistic
societies elsewhere as opposed to a more capitalistic economy here. In fact,
in 1980, the average pay for the CEOs of America's largest companies was
about forty times that of the average production worker. In 1990, that
multiple was eighty-five, and in 2003 it was four hundred.[3]

A mathematical formula known as the "Gini coefficient" measures
income disparity in a country or society.[4] In 2000, this index was greater
in the U.S. than in any European country or Canada. In fact, the coefficient for the U.S. was 40% higher than Canada. This disparity has remained
consistent since about 1980. As a result of this income gap, the difference
between the average physician salary and the average worker salary is higher
in the U.S. than in many other industrialized countries. In the U.S., this
spread was 5.5 times, compared to six European countries and Canada,
where the average spread was only 2.2 times. In Canada, the differential
was about 3.2 times.[5] Thus, the spread of salaries from low to high in most
industrialized countries is smaller than in the U.S.; therefore, the spread of
physicians' salaries compared to the average worker is likewise smaller in
other countries.

Another way to look at the issue of high physician income is to compare physician salaries to other similar occupations and professions to
determine if the wages are out of line. The U.S. National Compensation
Survey of July 2004, produced by the U.S. Department of Labor and the
Bureau of Labor Statistics yields the following excerpted table.[6]

	Mean hourly wage
All workers	$18.09
RN	$26.87
Pharmacist	$41.27
Dentist	$42.91
Advertising manager	$48.65
CEO public admin	$48.81
Lawyer	$48.89
University professor	$52.84
Medical science professor	$53.00
Judge	$56.14
Law professor	$57.05
Optometrist	$57.44
MD	$57.90
Economics professor	$63.98
Airline pilot	$113.82

The physician hourly wage appears to be in line and competitive with that of other professionals in this country. Considering the number of years of training, the expense of that training, and the large number of years expended until physicians are able to earn a reasonable income, the salary level does not appear unreasonable. A cardiologist will attend four years of college, four years of medical school, three years of internship and residency, and three to five years of cardiology fellowship for a total of fourteen to sixteen years of training beyond high school before he or she will be able to start employment at a reasonable salary. Approximately 81–85% of medical school graduates have debt with median amounts of $100,000 to $135,000, depending upon whether they attended public or private medical schools.[7] Additional debt is often incurred after medical school since the internship, residency, and fellowship salaries are often quite low. A comparison of educational costs and incomes for physicians, business people, attorneys, and dentists found that attorneys and business people had the highest rate of return on their educational investment. "Primary care physicians had the poorest financial results".[8] This financial reality translates to a greater than 50% decrease in the number of physicians entering family practice (primary care) training programs between 1997 and 2005.[9] If you think it is difficult to get an appointment to see your family doctor now, stick around; it will only get worse.

As a result of this analysis, one can conclude that physician salaries in the U.S. are high compared to other countries but are in line and reasonable by comparison to other professions in the U.S. As indicated previously, after correcting for PPP, U.S. physician salaries are 1.5 times higher than those in Canada.[10]

The other part of the salary expense equation is that of non-physician professional wages, such as those of nurses, technicians, pharmacists, dieticians, physical therapists, etc. Data from Canadian statistical databases and our National Compensation Survey shows that U.S. non-physician healthcare workers, on average, earn about 1.7 times more than their counterparts in Canada.[11, 12] The non-physician salaries are, once again, in line with other occupations in the U.S. Money-saving measures might exert a downward pressure on salaries, but with existing and projected shortages of physicians and skilled personnel, it is unlikely that this will happen. In fact, supply and demand logic would dictate a significant increase in these salaries over time!

Personnel Shortages

The Council on Graduate Medical Education, Bureau of Heath Professions, and numerous articles in lay and professional journals have predicted physician shortages from 50,000 to 230,000 by 2020. A national consulting firm, Merrit Hawkins, provided information from a 2003 survey indicating that 50% of physicians from age fifty to sixty-five planned to decrease significantly the scope of their practices or close them completely within the subsequent three years. They also indicated that it might take two younger physicians to replace a more senior physician since there are a larger number of younger female physicians who, on average, work about 18% fewer hours, and younger physicians, in general, expect to work fewer, more predictable hours with improved lifestyles.[13]

I see these changes occurring now, with many of my colleagues in their fifties looking to slow down significantly or completely retire as a result of frustration with the system and falling net revenues translating into lower salaries. With malpractice insurance premiums skyrocketing and fee schedules not keeping up with practice expenses or the cost of living, it is becoming almost impossible to work part-time as a consequence of high fixed expenses. Working full-time is also continuing to be a problem, with expenses rapidly outpacing the increases in fee schedules. The ever-increasing rules and regulations from insurance companies and the federal government add to the frustration. The constant arguing with insurers regarding pre-certification and justification for appropriate care of our patients and the effort spent to obtain proper payment is time consuming and wasteful. It is not uncommon for office staff and sometimes physicians themselves to spend thirty to sixty minutes on the phone trying to get permission to perform a study or to provide therapy for a patient.

Many physicians believe the insurers purposely place bureaucratic hurdles in front of physicians and patients so that we do not persist in efforts to obtain payment or care. I recently had a ninety-three-year-old patient in the hospital as a result of heart failure. She was living alone with some assistance from her family. With intravenous medical therapy, she became reasonably comfortable by the end of the second day and was out of bed, walking by the third day. She became lightheaded at the end of the third day with low blood pressure, and we had to decrease some of her medications to improve the situation. By the fourth day, she was walking fairly well with some assistance and was discharged home on the fifth day. She was insured by a private HMO, and it denied payment for the second through fifth days of her hospitalization, indicating that they were unnecessary. In its computerized set of rules for the treatment of heart failure, it only recognizes one hospital day for therapy; after that, the patient should be discharged. It would be difficult to do this for a younger patient and virtually impossible for a ninety-three-year-old one. The hospital and I spent about ten hours over the course of several weeks arguing with the insurance company for payment, at which point we were finally only partially successful. When I discussed the issue with the hospital CEO, he indicated that about 30% of the hospital days billed to private insurers were initially rejected and that efforts like this were needed to secure payments.

Unpleasant dealings with insurers have also undermined many doctor-patient relationships as a result of delays, wasted time, and unfulfilled expectations from both sides. These issues have caused a great deal of discontent within the medical community, and the dissatisfaction has become a frequent topic of conversation among physicians as well as the general public.

As a result of this and other issues, medical school applications fell by 28% from 1996 to 2002 and have just started a rise again in 2003–2005.[14] The possibility that we may have to lower the qualifications for medical school entry may become a reality if the number of applicants does not increase significantly in the near future. The "best and the brightest" may not be seeking careers in medicine but may be off to business and law schools. I have had the privilege of lecturing to classes in the Wharton Graduate MBA program. These young men and women were extremely bright and, in my opinion, at least some of them should have been sitting in a medical school classroom instead. Disappointingly, there were several young physicians in the class who were making career changes. Who will be taking care of our children and grandchildren when they get sick?

Physicians are not the only ones in short supply. There is a nursing shortage today, with estimates ranging from 10–20% of hospital positions vacant and an estimated 126,000 unfilled jobs in 2000. By 2020, there will be an estimated shortage of 800,000.[15, 16, 17, 18, 19] There is, likewise, a critical shortage of skilled medical, X-ray, and echocardiographic technicians and other healthcare personnel.

With more than 50% of the healthcare dollar going toward expenditures that directly involve intense professional care, the natural tendency to control costs would be to try to decrease them, in absolute terms, or reduce the growth of salaries.[20, 21] Attempts to control physician-related expenditures by reducing fee schedules or imposing strict budgetary restraints (as in Canada) will likely create increased dissatisfaction, resulting in more physicians leaving the profession prematurely and fewer bright people seeking a career in medicine. This would cause a further exacerbation of the shortage that is projected and seriously reduce access to care. There is now a six-week wait to see a physician in my practice for a routine new patient visit. Other groups in our area are experiencing the same problem. The demand for services in cardiology and most other medical specialties has grown dramatically over the past several years and will only continue to expand with the aging of the population and the baby boomers coming into their sixties.

The same principles hold true for nursing and other medical technology positions if we put unrealistic economic pressure on hospitals and the healthcare system in general. Nurses, in particular, are in such short supply that there is intense recruiting overseas, and it is not uncommon for hospitals to offer very large signing bonuses for nurses to join their staffs. Simple supply-and-demand relationships indicate that putting downward pressure on salaries will only intensify the existing and increasing shortages of trained personnel.

Price Controls

U.S. physicians are and have been operating under de facto *price control.* They have been fighting the battle for economic survival with one hand tied behind their backs. Let me elaborate. The Medicare system, which covers about forty-four million people, has a fee schedule for everything physicians do to and for the patient. There is no negotiation of this fee schedule, and it is manipulated by the federal government based upon a complex series of formulas in an effort to keep total expenses from increasing more than amounts established by law. In other words, if spending increases above the desired amount, the level of reimbursement per encounter falls. Furthermore, Medicare alters the amount paid for certain procedures to incentivize the use of lower-priced techniques. For example, it has decreased the reimbursement for open-heart surgery to make it less profitable for the hospitals and surgeons, thereby reducing the use of this procedure. If certain procedures are deemed to be over-utilized, Medicare adjusts the fees downward so that budget neutrality can be achieved. This is not a free market situation; it is total price control. If I were not to participate in the Medicare program and chose to bill Medicare patients directly for my services, federal law would prohibit me from billing for and collecting more than 115% of the Medicare fee schedule. End of discussion! Irrespective of how high my expenses escalate, I still cannot charge or collect more than 115% of the legislated fee schedule. As private insurance companies have gained market share across the country, they have adopted the Medicare fee schedule as a benchmark from which to decrease further their own payments to physicians. Not long ago, Medicare was considered the safety net of the elderly, and the reimbursements were fractions of what private insurers paid. All that has changed over the past seven to ten years, and in many instances the Medicare fee schedule is considered good reimbursement compared to that of many private insurers.

The rate of reimbursement from Medicare has not come close to keeping up with inflation, and, in many instances, the reimbursements have actually decreased significantly. In 1992, Medicare paid $2,559 for the surgeon's fee of an aortic valve replacement; by 2005 that figure had risen only to $2,740, a mere 7% increase. For stress testing, the 1992 payment was $112 and in 2005, $117, a 4% increase. For cardiac ultrasound, the figures are $269 in 1992 and $223 in 2005, a 17% decrease. Overall, from 1995 to 2003 the Medicare fee schedule increased by 13% while the inflation rate increased by 21%.[22]

Authoritative studies agree that physician fees for service and incomes have either decreased or have not kept pace with inflation.[23, 24] Furthermore, a survey published in the journal *Medical Economics* revealed average MD income growth from 1989 to 2002 was about 23% whereas the cost of living grew by 45%.[25] A study produced by a non-profit, non-partisan policy research organization found that physicians' income *decreased* by 7% after inflation adjustment from 1995 to 2003; other professional and technical workers *increased* by about 7%.[26]

Despite physician income lagging behind inflation for many years, the national Medicare expenditures have been outpacing governmental expectations. As a result, Medicare provided no cost of living increase to physicians' fees for 2007 and expects to reduce the fee schedule annually over the next six to eight years for a total of about a 30–40% decrease in income on top of a projected minimum 2–3% annual cost of living increase. The total net loss will be about 50% over this time frame.

The expenses for my practice are actually increasing by about 5% per year when you consider non-physician salaries, rent, supplies, malpractice costs, utilities, etc. This does not include the cost of purchasing and the start-up of a new multi-million dollar electronic medical record system over the next five years. With Medicare and only three major insurers in our region (Aetna, Independence Blue Cross of Pennsylvania, and Horizon of New Jersey), physicians are subjected to *de facto* price control. There is too much market consolidation for any physician to negotiate reimbursement enhancement effectively with any private insurer. All I see is my income being controlled, but not my expenses. Price control for physician income without price control for our expenses is not a long-term winning strategy for anyone. *This can only go on for so long before the net revenue to physicians is so low that huge numbers of bankruptcies will occur. Those who survive will come to the realization that it is no longer worth it— physicians will retire early; fewer college graduates will apply to medical schools; the quality of the physician work force will decrease; quality of care will erode; and greater discontent will breed poor doctor-patient relationships.*

Uncompensated Professional Time

I believe an argument can be made that physician fees are a bargain when you consider how much time and service we provide for no payment. We do not typically speak about these free services; but since we are discussing salaries and expenses, it seems appropriate to deal with these issues now.

With forty-eight million uninsured people in the U.S. in 2006, physicians generally provide their care for free. This amounted to about $5 billion in 2001, the last year for this data.[27] The uninsured typically do not have the resources to pay us, and therefore billing them or even suing them yields little, if any, payment. We oftentimes do not even bother to pursue collection attempts after billing them once or twice. It usually costs more than the actual receipts. Our group practices at nine hospitals, two of which are tertiary care institutions in the inner city. Virtually every day we provide care for several new patients, as well as patients we have already seen in the past, with no insurance, knowing that we will likely never see any revenue.

Recently, I was called at 2 A.M. to see a patient complaining of chest pain at the emergency room of one of the tertiary care hospitals. I was told that he had no insurance. After evaluating him, I thought he had a dissecting aortic aneurysm (a tear in the major blood vessel that comes out of the heart) and performed a special test involving passing a device into his esophagus to take pictures of the torn artery. It confirmed the diagnosis. I started emergency medications and called a heart surgeon to have him operated upon as an emergency since this problem is immediately life threatening. I stayed with him for about an hour, waiting for the surgeon and operating room staff to come in and get him to the operating room to be sure that he remained stable. He had successful surgery, which saved his life, and he was home in about five days. While waiting for the surgeon, he and I chatted, and he mentioned to me that he had no insurance, which I knew from the outset. He had a good job, but he declined health insurance since it would have cost him several thousand dollars per year to cover himself and his family. He used that money to take vacations. He never paid the surgeon or me for our services. This is a common scenario we face every day with the indigent, the working poor, and people who decide they do not need insurance.

Another issue is Medicaid, which covered about fifty-four million Americans in 2006. The fee schedule for Medicaid is about 60% of Medicare and sometimes less.[28] For those of us who practice in or near inner cities or in other regions that have a high indigent population, such as the rural U.S., we provide care for very little compensation. Our practice has about a 7% Medicaid population. We never turn away a patient, and since many other cardiologists in our region have chosen not to see these patients, we service the vast majority of them. These patients often have advanced disease and require a very high level of complicated care, which we provide daily with a huge discount.

The uninsured and the underinsured are not the only groups of patients for whom we provide free service daily. For patients of ours who have insurance, we fill out insurance forms, disability forms, duplicate prescriptions for mail-in drug companies, write letters to insurance companies in support of patients to obtain authorization for care, and perform many other administrative services for free. An attorney or accountant would certainly charge and receive payment for these services.

It is not uncommon for us to discuss cases with our partners or other physicians in different specialties in order to provide the best care possible. My attorney and accountant charge for the time they spend discussing my issues with their associates. Physicians, in general, can only charge for face-to-face encounters with patients.

Another example of uncompensated work is time we spend dealing with anticoagulant (blood thinner) management. Patients who are taking warfarin (coumadin) require relatively frequent blood tests to control the level of the drug in their blood. This drug is potentially dangerous and requires meticulous management. We average about one thousand encounters per month that require our personnel to receive the test results from the labs, archive them, discuss the result with a physician, and then call the patient with instructions. Each transaction takes about ten minutes and consumes the time of one technician, costing us about $40,000 per year including benefits, plus physician time, all of which is totally without compensation. Nationally, there are about four million patients taking this type of blood thinner who require blood testing and analysis.[29] On average, tests are required one to three times a month, depending upon the stability of the patient. This translates to about 50–150 million tests per year, generally for no compensation. There is no reimbursement for this service, yet it is vital for the health of many of our patients.

One might think that bad debt (unpaid bills) would somehow be tax deductible as it is in other businesses. In medicine, however, this is not the case. So, therefore, not only do we provide a substantial amount of free services to the insured and uninsured, for which we are exposed to a significant malpractice risk, but we also have no tax benefit for bad debt.

I would like to discuss the work involved when physicians are "on call". This is usually not included in the computation of the hours we work. I am not sure why this is; but for many specialties, like cardiology, it is a major part of our work-week. In our group, as in most others, each cardiologist takes "call" about one night a week and one weekend per month. We do not receive compensation time off after we have been on call. This means that we work the entire day, take call that night, and then work the next day as well. When we work the weekend, we likewise do not have compensation time off. This means that we work the entire week and the next week as well, or twelve days in a row. The weekend call for us and most specialists entails making rounds at the hospitals, caring for our patients who are there, and dealing with emergencies who get admitted, often without medical insurance. We also take all the calls from our patients who are not hospitalized and have questions or concerns about their health.

We work about six to eight hours each weekend day and also take calls at night. The phone calls at night (weekday or weekend) are calls from nurses regarding patients in the various hospitals; from non-hospitalized patients who have questions about medications, test results, symptoms such as chest pain or shortness of breath, or who are requesting appointments; and from people seeking information about their loved ones who are hospitalized. Many of these calls from patients should have occurred during the day when office staff is available to help handle the issues, but for some reason patients often choose to call at night. Nighttime on call starts at about 5 P.M., when our offices close, and goes to 7 A.M. the next morning. We receive about twenty calls from 5 P.M. to midnight and about five to ten calls after midnight. We don't get much sleep! Furthermore, about every other call night we must actually go to the hospital to see a very sick patient or perform a cardiac catheterization or some other procedure on a critically ill patient. Bear in mind that through all of this, we always go to work the next day and have a full day of patient care. The only time we receive any compensation for this effort is when we see a patient face to face. All the phone calls are free!!

It is not uncommon to receive phone calls from patients about non-life-threatening problems after midnight. A sample call goes something like this: The patient tells me that he has swelling of his ankles. "How long have you had this problem?" I ask. "About three weeks," he states. "Is it any worse now?" "No," he responds. "How severe is the swelling?" He states, "My ankles seem to flop over my shoes by the end of the day, but are okay in the morning." I inquire if he has any shortness of breath or chest pain, and he says, "No." We go over his medications, and I make an adjustment of his water pill and ask him to call the office in a few days, during the day! Since the patient or his insurance company does not pay for this service, there is no expense for him to make the call. The patient could have and should have waited for the office to open in the morning. I doubt many of these patients would even consider calling their attorneys at 3 A.M. to discuss a non-emergency problem. And if they did call, at any time, they would expect to get a bill. There is certainly a double-edged sword here, however. If there were a significant charge for these phone calls, it is possible that truly sick patients might not call as readily and therefore get sicker or worse, but the non-emergency calls would be curtailed. Some reasonable compromise is needed.

All physicians know, early in their training, that night call "comes with the territory". Anytime a life can be saved or suffering can be reduced, we don't hesitate to respond. In the end, however, physicians (and their spouses) are the ones who lose sleep and receive no compensation for it. Being on-call is a major reason physicians leave their practices, and it is a significant deciding factor as to what specialty new physicians choose.

I have several friends who are businessmen and think physicians are crazy for providing these free services and treating uninsured and Medicaid patients the way we do. They believe that "if you cannot pay, you should not play" and that these patients should be denied care. I then feel compelled to discuss the Hippocratic Oath, compassion, public service, doing the right thing—all to no avail. They counter with, "How long can a grocery store afford to allow people to take food without paying or paying twenty-five to fifty cents on the dollar?" Frankly, no business or profession would permit this type of behavior. The medical profession permits this every day and night without anyone standing up and making the case that there needs to be recognition and repair of the situation.

To Sum Up:

- Salaries account for more than 50% of the costs of the healthcare system.
- Physician and non-physician professional salaries appear to be in line with other similar professions in the U.S.
- There is an existing shortage of nurses and a growing severe shortage on the horizon that will dictate significantly increasing salaries for the foreseeable future. A similar trend is likely for other non-physician healthcare professionals.
- Serious physician shortages are predicted for the future, which will compound existing regional shortages, making it difficult to reduce fees for service and physician income significantly without further reducing the number of physicians. Access to care and the quality of care could be markedly reduced in the years to come.
- Therefore, it is unlikely that anything of *significance* can be done to reduce costs of professional services appreciably by reducing fee schedules without severe damage to the healthcare system now and for the foreseeable future.
- Physicians currently provide care for the uninsured, underinsured, and Medicaid population for little or no payment.
- Physicians provide many necessary services to patients with and without insurance for which they are generally not compensated.

- Physician income has been curtailed by *de facto* price control while expenses have increased significantly.
- Physicians generally have no negotiating power over reimbursements since insurers have too much market consolidation and control. Medicare and Medicaid fee schedules are non-negotiable, low, and not keeping up with the cost of living.
- Medicare, Medicaid, and the uninsured make up about *one half* of the U.S. population.
- Make no mistake: The poor reimbursement policies of this country are creating a very serious crisis wherein quality professionals are leaving healthcare and young men and women are not choosing to enter. We will all pay the price for this.

CHAPTER 3

Hospitals—The Expensive "Court of Last Resort"

Hospital finances are at best tenuous, and it is doubtful that significant cuts in reimbursement will be possible without serious damage to these institutions. We will analyze the economics of hospitals to determine why the costs are high and why they are unlikely to be reduced in any meaningful way in the foreseeable future.

Similar to the physician's dilemma regarding the care of the uninsured and the Medicaid patients, hospitals cannot refuse care to anyone who arrives at the emergency room. Therefore, hospitals must incur all the costs of care, often with expectations of minimal or no payment. Additionally, Medicare has been cutting reimbursement to such an extent that hospitals are now losing money on the elderly population.

The Expense Side

Seventy percent of hospital expenses are for salaries and benefits.[1] In the chapter on physicians, we discussed the fact that salaries for physicians and other healthcare workers are in line with their counterparts in non-healthcare occupations. If the revenue of hospitals were to decrease significantly as a result of Medicare, Medicaid, and other insurers ratcheting down payments, salaries would have to be cut. If this were to occur, we would see an exodus of qualified workers to other occupations. Several years ago, when salaries did not keep pace with inflation, there was a migration of nurses from many of the hospitals in southern New Jersey to work in Atlantic City casinos as blackjack dealers. This problem was resolved by offering the nurses large increases in salaries, signing bonuses, and other inducements to return. With existing and anticipated shortages of nurses, physicians, and other technical workers, there would be a major collapse of the hospital system if salaries were not competitive. Alternatively, less qualified people could be hired for less money, making the system unsafe. This is not theory; it is a real possibility, and to some extent it is happening now. In many hospitals, workers are being cross-trained to do several jobs, such as mop the floor and take blood pressures. The ability of these people to do this type of diverse work is, at best, questionable and, at worst, puts patients in jeopardy.

So if salaries really cannot be reduced, can we decrease the number of workers, such as nurses, X-ray technicians, orderlies, dieticians, etc.? Hospitals provide costly and extremely labor-intensive services. Many intensive care units have one RN for each patient around the clock every day, plus support staff. This is very expensive, and, with the shortage of nurses, this necessary staffing ratio has caused beds to remain empty. When hospital beds cannot be staffed, patients in emergency rooms cannot be moved out to appropriate beds, and the ER becomes full and must close its doors to new patients. Every city faces this problem continuously, and a major reason for ER closure is lack of hospital bed availability, often as a result of nursing shortages. A Massachusetts report indicated that there were 11,124 hours of diversion (hours of closed emergency rooms) in the state during the first nine months of 2005, up about 10% from 2004.[2] Additionally, scheduled surgical procedures are often canceled for lack of bed availability. This is extremely disruptive for patients, who are psychologically ready for surgery, and for their caregivers, who often have taken a day off from work.

The most frequent complaint heard from patients, physicians, and nurses alike concerns the lack of adequate numbers of skilled personnel. The American Hospital Association estimated, in an April 2006 survey, that there is a shortage of 118,000 RNs for an 8.5% vacancy rate nationwide. Eighty-five percent of hospital CEOs reported a nursing shortage in a 2005 survey by the American College of Health Executives. Those of us who work in hospitals know this is indeed the case. A study from the

University of Pennsylvania found that twenty thousand patients die each year when they are hospitalized in an institution with overworked nurses, and there is a 31% greater risk of dying if a nursing shortage exists in your hospital. Additionally, it is estimated that four million hospital days are wasted each year as a direct result of nursing shortages.[3, 4]

Nursing is a vital part of the healthcare equation and should not be underestimated. Aside from playing a crucial role in nurturing and caring, nurses are highly technically trained to deal with sophisticated problems of drug administration and intensive care unit management of critically ill patients; they are also advocates for patients who are unable to express themselves. It is not uncommon for a nurse to supply insight into the interactions of patients and their families, enabling physicians to see the entire picture of a patient's health status.

There is a patient of mine, Marian, who was about eighty-five years old and was hospitalized for heart failure for the third time in three months. It was difficult to understand why she was not doing well, since she told me she was eating properly and taking her medications as prescribed. I was very concerned that we were missing something. Then one of her nurses in the hospital told me that Marian confided to her that she could not read and was depending upon her family to give her the correct medicines. Marian was also worried that her family did not care enough to be diligent about her dosing. We were finally able to get the problem resolved by having Marian live with another daughter, and she has not been in the hospital for more than a year. This is one simple example of how patients will confide in a caring nurse and tell her or him things they will not otherwise reveal. This can make a great difference in the welfare and treatment of the patient.

Many states mandate minimum staffing ratios for various parts of the hospital, including intensive care units and regular medical floors, in an effort to protect the public from understaffing in situations where hospital budgetary constraints may entice administrators to cut nursing and other support positions. Most of us would agree that hospitals have a shortage of staff to begin with. All you have to do is push the call button to summon a nurse or orderly and you will be a believer that there really is a shortage. Try getting off the bedpan by yourself. Furthermore, nurses and other skilled personnel are complaining that they are overworked and asked to do mandatory overtime and to perform jobs that are not really meant for them to do. These are major causes of burnout and career changes.

So if salaries and the number of workers cannot be reduced, the next possibility is to reduce the cost of drugs and medical devices. We will discuss these costs in a later chapter, but the short story is that hospitals do not have enough bargaining power with pharmaceutical and device companies to get significant price reductions, as compared to pricing in other countries. Furthermore, many new drugs (antibiotics, clot busters, cancer chemotherapy, etc.) are developed annually that are lifesaving and are needed by hospitalized patients. These new drugs are on patent for many years, so there is no generic and only minimal price flexibility from the manufacturer.

The remaining 23% of hospital costs (after salaries and drugs/devices) includes malpractice insurance, administrative expenses, utilities, food, chemicals, postage, uniforms, patient gowns, laundry, and a few other items. The prices of most of these items are either not negotiable or will yield minimal savings. There is really no leeway to reduce hospital expenses by any meaningful amount.

The Revenue Side

Leaving the expense side of the equation and turning to the revenue side is even more frustrating.

Hospitals have been losing money for the care of Medicare and Medicaid patients in increasing amounts from 1999 to 2004. In 2004, national losses exceeded $22 billion in aggregate. As a result of decreased governmental reimbursement, 68% of hospitals lost money on Medicare and/or Medicaid patients, and one-third lost money overall in 2004.[5] These losses, in addition to the losses from uninsured patients ($27 billion in 2004 or 5.6% of total hospital expenses),[6] have prompted most hospitals to attempt to obtain higher reimbursement from private insurers in an effort to break even. When this is not successful, in regions where the private insurers are very powerful, the hospitals lose money overall. When this is successful, those of us purchasing private health insurance see our premiums increase. So not only are you paying federal and state taxes to run Medicaid and Medicare programs and state taxes to pay for charity care, which covers some of the uninsured hospital expense, you are also paying higher private insurance premiums to offset a portion of hospital losses. Wouldn't it be better to fund the Medicare/Medicaid costs properly and not to shift the burden to those of us who pay for private insurance? More about the insurance companies later.

Advertising

One other small point is the need, or perceived need, for hospitals to advertise. The competition among hospitals in many regions of the country, especially large cities, is fierce. As a result, they are spending increasing amounts of money for advertising. We see it in television and radio commercials, newspaper ads, mailings, and brochures. In 2001, annual advertising expenditures were about $500 million and in 2005, $810 million. On average, a two-hundred to four-hundred bed hospital spent about $1.24 million in 2004.[7] This is not a huge amount of money compared to a total hospital annual expenditure in excess of $200 million, but it could pay the salaries of more nurses and other support personnel, who are desperately needed.

Efficiency: The Holy Grail

The only real way to cut expenses is to decrease further the lengths of stay without harming the patient and without premature discharge that will cause readmissions. The best way to accomplish this is to enable the patient to have several diagnostic and/or therapeutic procedures performed daily, as tolerated by the patient's condition. The most important contribution of the HMOs and the managed care system is that they mandated better use of each hospital day, so that more was accomplished and the length of stay was reduced. This was not altruism, but rather a good economic strategy that allowed the insurance companies to pay less for hospitalizations since the lengths of stay were shortened. In fact, in 1980, the length of stay on average was 7.5 days, and in 2003 it was 4.8 days.[8]

I can recall when I was in medical school in the late sixties that a person with a heart attack was hospitalized for about three weeks. Now, that same patient will be in the hospital for about four days, and, at times, one day if he has a successful angioplasty on admission and we can abort much of the damage. Total inpatient hospital days dropped from 280 million to about 200 million per year during the same period of time (1980–2003) despite a growing and aging population.[9] The Canadian length of stay was about 6.9 days in 2003.[10] The difference between 6.9 and 4.8 days is enormous when it comes to costs. Hospitals can care for significantly more patients without increasing staffing, thereby increasing gross and net revenue.

In 2003, the per capita hospital expense in Canada was $951 PPP vs. $1,774 in the U.S. The length of stay in the U.S. was about 30% less than that in Canada, but the number of hospitalizations per one hundred people was about 50% higher in the U.S. (8.4 in Canada vs. 12 in the U.S.). If we multiply admissions per one hundred people times the average length of stay per admission for each country, we come up with about fifty-seven hospital days per one hundred people per year in each country. With the number of hospital days per one hundred people the same in each country and the costs in the U.S. about twice that of Canada, it is clear that the excess expense in the U.S. is a result of costs per day. Seventy-seven percent of the expense is salary and drugs/devices. Since we probably cannot meaningfully reduce salaries or the costs of drugs and devices (as noted previously, hospitals have little bargaining power with drug and device manufacturers) and the other 23% of the expense is, as we saw, likewise relatively fixed, the best way to save additional money is to improve the efficiency of care by doing more per day to decrease further the lengths of stay.

So how can we continue to shorten this most important parameter? We need physicians to become more involved with patient care multiple times a day. Ordinarily, in non-critical care units a doctor will see a patient once a day and prescribe a series of drugs or tests to be performed. Then he or she will not interact with the patient again until the next day, unless there is an urgent issue that requires his or her attention. Most tests to diagnose illnesses are based upon the results of other tests and are done in sequence. If physicians were able to obtain the results of tests performed during the early part of the day, it is likely that additional studies could be ordered and performed that same day. It might also be possible for a third round of tests to be performed the same day, thereby, in many instances, shortening three days into one.

We have done this frequently in our practice. An example is a patient admitted to the hospital in the morning for chest pain. On day one, several blood tests and EKGs could rule out a heart attack. On day two, a stress test would be performed, and, if the results were normal, the patient would be discharged from the hospital. If all these tests were done in sequence on day one, the hospitalization would be cut by one day. Or if the tests were performed while the patient were still in the emergency room and if the tests were normal, the hospitalization could be avoided completely. Alternatively, if the stress test were abnormal, the patient could immediately undergo cardiac catheterization and, if necessary, an angioplasty, allowing the patient to be discharged the next day. This would shorten a four-day hospitalization to one overnight stay.

The only way this can be done is if the physician is present in the hospital all day or is available to review the test results and if the facilities can handle this rapid turnover. In general, this requires fast turnaround of X-ray and lab reports, an information system geared to producing these reports quickly, often without transcription costs and delays; attending physicians receiving the reports immediately and then being able to respond by ordering new tests; and nurses receiving the orders and having the staffing to get the next study done promptly. It takes great effort on the part of many people and is almost Herculean in nature. It is currently being done in a few settings with cooperation, incentives, and with significant investment in computer infrastructure, both in the hospitals and in physician offices. Some hospitals have hired "hospitalists" who only care for inpatients and are expected to be able to focus all of their efforts on expediting the care of these patients without office responsibilities. The theory is that they can see these patients multiple times per day and shorten the lengths of stay while providing appropriate care. The studies looking at this type of program are mixed as to the benefits and disadvantages.

Wouldn't it be great if hospital test results could appear in real time on a physician's computer in his office or on his "Blackberry", which would then allow him to order the next test by computer as well? This could occur several times per day for each patient, thereby reducing the length of hospital stay. Since this would involve significant extra time, physicians would be compensated for their efforts and incentivized to accomplish these essential goals. With reimbursements not keeping pace with inflation and the anticipated Medicare fee schedule reductions, however, there is less motivation for physicians to do extra work. Hospitals would also need to make an enormous multimillion-dollar investment in order to accomplish this. Unfortunately, as previously stated, there is no extra money in the hospital budgets.

The federal government needs to step up and commit billions of dollars annually to help build and maintain this technology network. An annual investment of $10 billion would represent about .5% of the total healthcare expenditure. Sometimes you need to spend some money to save in the long run!

To Sum Up:

- We spend about twice the per capita cost compared to Canada for hospital care while using the same number of hospital days per one hundred people.
- The financial health of hospitals is poor as a result of insufficient reimbursements, in part mandated by the government (Medicare and Medicaid), and low revenues from private insurers in regions with a few dominant companies that can control the market.
- There needs to be a more realistic reimbursement system for hospitals that funds them appropriately and provides money for purchasing the means to be more efficient and improve quality.
- Seventy percent of hospital expenses comes from salaries. The existing and future shortage of nurses and skilled personnel makes it impossible to cut salaries. State staffing mandates and good medical care make it impossible to reduce the number of skilled employees to decrease expenses.
- The cost of drugs and devices (about 7% of total hospital expenses) is generally minimally negotiable since the most effective drugs and devices are still on patent.
- The only real way to reduce the cost of hospital care is by improving the efficiency of the use of each hospital day. This is very difficult and will cost substantial dollars in infrastructure. Federal, state, and regional governments are awakening to the need to finance these improvements and, in some instances, are partnering with private insurers to bring additional dollars to support this investment. Hospitals are also partnering with large technology companies, such as GE and Siemens, to develop systems that will improve efficiency. With more widespread adoption of these systems, the costs will decrease and allow more hospitals to partake in the transformation to greater safety and cost effectiveness.

CHAPTER 4

Private Insurance—Caring for Profit

Background

In 1973, the Health Maintenance Organization Act created an insurance system whereby patients could pay a premium to a federally approved insurance company and receive care from their panel of physicians and hospitals preselected by the company generally based upon negotiated pricing. The patient was assigned a primary care physician (PCP) who acted as a gatekeeper through whom any tests, referrals to specialists, and hospitalizations would have to be approved. In exchange for this level of control, the patient was given a lower premium than he or she was paying for standard indemnity insurance where no controls existed.

This system of coverage caught on at various speeds in different parts of the country. It was very widely accepted in California and became the basis of much of its healthcare insurance. It spread to other areas of the country and morphed into less restrictive plans known as Preferred Provider Organizations (PPOs) and Point of Service (POS) care depending upon market acceptance and needs as assessed by the parent insurance organizations. An in-depth analysis of these various organizations is not possible in this book. Suffice it to say that the underlying premise of these entities has been to bring down the cost of care or at least to reduce the rate of annual increases. These HMO plans were quite effective during the early and mid-1990s, but, by the year 2000, the rate of increase of costs was once again higher than general inflation.

The most effective mechanism used by the insurance companies was to demand shorter hospital stays by using a series of tables compiled by consulting companies that defined how long someone should be in the hospital based upon his or her admission diagnosis. The insurance companies would then disallow payment for any and all days beyond that point, unless there was a very good reason for the "delay" in discharge. This was extremely effective in making hospitals and physicians look carefully at what was accomplished each day and in making sure that no delays took place. This was not a perfect system, but it certainly made physicians and hospitals function differently.

The system also required preauthorization for certain expensive tests and for any admissions other than emergencies. We learned how to do outpatient cardiac catheterizations and pacemaker insertions, shortened the hospital stay for a heart attack from three weeks to about three to five days, and learned how to perform a whole host of surgical procedures without admitting patients to hospitals.

Many of these advances occurred as a result of new and improved technology, but it is likely that a major impetus to create these new techniques was a direct result of the pressure exerted by the managed care companies. I can recall having endless meetings with hospital administrators, nurses, other physicians, and ancillary personnel to devise and implement techniques to reduce lengths of stay. We met with success in most instances and gradually saw overall decreases in hospital days. This was a very good thing that would not have happened without the prodding and financial penalties imposed by the insurance companies. However, they did not offer any insight into how to accomplish these efficiencies. It was completely an issue of constant economic persuasion. In general, most of the reductions of hospital days were safe and reasonable and involved decreasing waste. We all remember some of the problems, however, such as "drive thru deliveries," where mothers would be in the hospital for less than twenty-four hours after giving birth.

At the outset of the managed care "revolution," I, as the managing partner of a large cardiology group, attended numerous meetings with founders and senior executives of several HMOs that were trying to start up in southern New Jersey. I can tell you that, in the beginning, the HMOs had no idea how to bring down costs, except to act as a bully by denying virtually every request that came to them for non-emergency care with the hopes that some of the requests would disappear, which they did. They admitted this to me at several meetings, and it became obvious when dealing with them. The adage that these companies "manage money and not care" was and is true from my vantage point and from that of nearly all other physicians regardless of specialty or years in practice.

As time went by, however, the HMOs became more sophisticated, with better computerization and statistical analysis. Many consulting companies sprang up to analyze hospital admission data and practice profiles to try to determine which practices were performing in a cost-effective manner. This is, at best, an inexact science. They are still in the business of denying care; but now they are using guidelines that are, in some instances, based upon accepted practice protocols. In many instances, their decisions regarding accepted lengths of stay are still arbitrary and capricious. The example of the ninety-three-year-old lady with heart failure, discussed in a previous chapter, is merely one of many instances of abusive denials. I have yet to receive any clinical advice on how to improve the inpatient care of my patients from any of the dozens of managed care companies with which I deal. One would think that, with all the data and resources these companies have, they would be able to document "best practice protocols" and share them with physicians and hospitals to improve healthcare and efficiency. I have not seen this yet.

Another means by which these companies saved money was by withholding payments to physicians and hospitals on a regular basis. This, in general, has been less of a problem over the past several years, but it took state-sponsored legislation to accomplish this. Reduction in payments also occurred in the past and continues to be a serious problem as a result of the carriers bundling together various procedures and only paying for one of them. The HMOs often do not follow accepted standards, such as the Medicare system, and make up these bundling policies without supportive logic. For example, a nuclear imaging stress test has about five components recognized by Medicare and the AMA council, which oversees procedure nomenclature. Some private insurers with significant market clout have bundled two or three of these components into one, thus reducing the overall reimbursement. As a consequence, they are paying a much smaller amount for the entire study than if they paid for all the components. The savings to the insurers can amount to one-third or more of the total fee. Some of these reductions have been reversed as a result of a lengthy class action lawsuit with a settlement between state medical societies and several of the major insurance companies.

An example of persistent waste in the managed care system is demonstrated by an interesting conversation I had several years ago with the senior medical director of one of the largest managed care companies in New Jersey. I pointed out to him that our group had virtually never been denied permission to perform any test on any patient insured by his company since we follow accepted guidelines. As a result, I asked him if we could eliminate the preauthorization process and thereby save our group and his company significant time and money. He said he would check with the company and try to verify my assertion. We met again about a month later (nothing happens quickly), and he said he had indeed verified my assertion, but his "company would not be a managed care company if it did not manage the care of its subscribers, so the answer is no." This seems crazy in view of our track record of no denials and the mutual benefit of reducing delays and costs.

Using the above as a prelude, I will now begin to discuss the economics of these health insurance companies to give you some insights into how they function.

The "Six-Hundred-Pound Gorilla"

Managed care companies rose to prominence over the past thirty years and in 2004 were so dominant that they controlled the healthcare market in virtually all—279 of 296—major metropolitan areas in the country, as defined by the Department of Justice. This meant that any two companies controlled greater than 50% of the healthcare insurance in each of these regions. Furthermore, in 280 regions at least one company controlled 30% or more of the market share. In over half the regions, one company controlled more than 50% of the market, and in about 20% of the markets one company had at least a 70% market share.[1] As a consequence of this dominance, it has become virtually impossible for physicians to negotiate fee schedules. Hospitals have had to merge in order to become strong enough to get a seat at the table and gain some bargaining power. In 2004, for example, 236 hospitals nationwide merged.[2]

In our region of southern New Jersey, three companies have gained control of the market. They are Aetna, Horizon Blue Cross and Blue Shield, and Amerihealth, which is a subsidiary of Independence Blue Cross of Philadelphia. They each control about a third of the non-Medicare market. It would be extremely difficult to threaten to walk away from them in an effort to exert bargaining pressure. With Medicare and Medicaid fee schedules being non-negotiable and the private insurers so dominant in our market and 95% of the major metropolitan markets in the U.S., physicians are stuck with virtual price control for reimbursements.

This relative monopsony (insurance companies are the buyers of medical services from hospitals and physicians) has allowed the carriers to dictate compensation and, to a lesser extent, premiums.[3] They still have to compete with one another for patients. In order to achieve these dominant positions, insurance companies have also consolidated. Between 1999 and 2003, there was a 30% decrease in the number of carriers, fueling this growing market monopsony.[4]

Capitalism vs. Greed

Several insurance companies have become so large and so dominant through mergers and acquisitions that they are now reaping huge profits for their shareholders.[5]

	2004 revenue in billions	2005 revenue in billions	2004 earnings in billions	2005 earnings in billions	2004 MLR	2005 MLR
Aetna	$19.90	$22.50	$2.30	$1.60	77.8%	76.9%
Cigna	$18.20	$16.70	$1.40	$1.60	82.4%	82.3%
Healthnet	$11.60	$11.90	$0.04	$0.23	88.0%	83.9%
Humana	$13.10	$14.40	$0.05	$0.07	84.1%	83.2%
UnitedHealth	$37.20	$45.40	$2.60	$3.30	80.2%	78.6%
Wellpoint	$20.80	$45.10	$0.96	$2.50	82.0%	80.6%
Totals	$120.80	$156.00	$7.35	$9.29		
Mean					82.4%	80.9%

Insurance companies collect premiums and spend a portion of the proceeds on medical care. The medical expenses paid on behalf of the subscribers divided by the revenues (premiums) are known as the "medical loss ratios" or MLR. Because this had an unsavory connotation, the insurers changed the term to "medical expense ratio". The lower the number, the higher the profit. As indicated above in the chart, the average spent on medical care in 2005 was about 81%, with the remainder spent on administration, office buildings, computers, salaries for the senior executives, advertising, lawyers, accountants, and profit going to the shareholders. A 2003 study reported the average of the eleven highest annual CEO salaries was $15 million, with the highest going to Norman Payson of Oxford Health Plans at $76 million. The average of the unexercised stock options was $67 million, with the highest being $530 million for William McGuire of United Health.[6] McGuire was forced to resign as CEO in 2006 because of a stock option scandal that could cost the company $1.7 billion to correct, according to Associated Press reports.

The goal of these publicly traded companies is to make money for their shareholders, and healthcare coverage is just the vehicle to accomplish this. The average HMO operating margin (profit) was about 3.5% in 2004, while the largest insurers brought in between 8% and 13%.[7, 8] Though the percentage is modest, the amount in actual dollars is huge and could go a long way toward reducing premiums, enhancing benefits, or providing insurance to the uninsured.

A recent study found that nine of the largest U.S. private health insurance companies employed between 13.7 and 35.1 people per ten thousand enrollees, compared to about 1.3 employees per ten thousand enrollees in the Canadian National Health Plans.[9] This staggering difference in employment—and therefore costs—is problematic and should not go unnoticed.

In 2004, the total national expenditure for private heath insurance was about $658 billion.[10] The 20% overhead of these companies amounts to $132 billion. If all private carriers had overhead similar to Medicare (1.8%),[11, 12] the cost of administering the private health sector would be about $12 billion, and the savings would be about $120 billion annually. Keep this number in mind as we will come back to it later. This savings could be applied toward the provision of healthcare to the uninsured or to the reduction of premiums or both, which would resolve the issue of obtaining health coverage for the forty-eight million uninsured and still leave money for reduction of premiums. Obviously, the money from the private insurance savings would not be applied directly to the uninsured, but it could be redirected by changes in taxation policy. The bottom line is that the money is available in the current system.

The "Not-for-Profit" Myth

Private insurance companies are either for-profit or non-profit. One might think the non-profits would have a different expense profile and use the premium dollar in a more efficient manner to provide more care and less "profit". This is not at all the case. A 2003 report by a well-respected consulting company (Milliman U.S.A.), published online by the non-profit Blue Cross Blue Shield Association, demonstrated that the medical loss ratio, administrative costs, and "profit" for the association's member plans nationwide were almost exactly the same as for the for-profit insurance companies.[13] The huge "profits" are held in reserve as a "rainy-day fund" by the non-profit companies. Hard to believe, but true.

The healthcare dollar should be sacred and should be used for providing care and nothing else!

The Premium Escalation

Despite large dollar profits, the private insurance companies (for-profit and non-profit) have raised premiums dramatically over the past several years. The premiums have exceeded the net healthcare cost increases significantly in five of the past seven years and have surpassed the Consumer Price Index (CPI) by a factor of almost four times. The average premium increase was almost 2.3% above the "net" total healthcare expense increases, and one year it was greater than 6% higher in absolute terms. It is not difficult to determine why the premiums have increased faster than healthcare expenses. These private insurers have huge overheads in salaries/benefits, real estate, etc., which go up annually, and there is the overriding need to show profit for the shareholders. The companies have raised and will likely continue to raise premiums to whatever the "traffic will bear" in order to cover overhead and maximize profits. To the extent that they are private companies, they are not compelled to adhere to precepts of the public welfare and are not controlled like public utilities, such as electricity, water, telephone, and public transportation. They can charge whatever they believe they can get away with. Local competition with other insurers is their only impediment to rising premiums. The following chart demonstrates that the average increase in yearly insurance premiums has been about 32% higher than the increases in the "net" healthcare costs. In some years, the increases were almost twice as much as those of the cost of healthcare. Furthermore, the average premium grew almost four times as fast as the CPI over this seven-year period.[14, 15, 16]

	Total national HC expense in billions	% yearly increase in total HC expense	"Net" increase in HC expense (Total HC expense increase minus pop growth	% yearly increase in private insurance premiums	Annual CPI increase
1998	$1,150	5.41%	4.41%	3.70%	1.60%
1999	$1,216	5.74%	4.74%	4.80%	2.20%
2000	$1,300	6.91%	5.91%	8.30%	3.40%
2001	$1,413	8.70%	7.70%	11.00%	2.80%
2002	$1,607	13.73%	12.73%	12.70%	1.60%
2003	$1,740	8.28%	7.28%	13.90%	2.30%
2004	$1,877	7.87%	6.87%	11.20%	2.70%
Average		8.09%	7.09%	9.37%	2.37%

Our practice, for instance, has had 10–27% increases in our healthcare premiums to insure our employees annually over the past five years. These increases are despite higher deductibles and copayments causing workers to spend greater amounts of money out-of-pocket. We have tried to keep the employee dollar contribution to their health insurance premiums fairly stable over the past seven to eight years by absorbing the excess premium costs and shopping around for more affordable coverage, often with fewer benefits or higher copayments. This is becoming more of a struggle, however, and we will likely have to raise the amount our employees pay monthly.

Nationwide, the average employee contribution has increased from $30 to $51 per month from 2001 to 2005 despite higher deductibles and copayments.

So what bottom-line fiscal conclusions can we draw from this analysis?

- Managed care companies have played a key role in reducing waste in the healthcare system. This dramatically reduced healthcare cost increases in the 1990s.

- Insurance companies generally manage money, not care.
- Insurers have gained competitive control of almost all of the healthcare markets in the country, thereby allowing them to dictate reimbursement to physicians and, to a lesser extent, hospitals.
- Insurance premiums have increased much faster than the Consumer Price Index (CPI) and the total national healthcare expense.
- Insurers (for-profit and non-profit) are enjoying large "profits".
- CEO salaries and stock options are enormous.
- The cost of private health insurance overhead, including profit, is enormous compared to Medicare (20% vs. 1.8%).
- If the insurance companies had an overhead similar to Medicare, there would be about $120 billion per year that could be spent on the uninsured, and there would still be money left over to reduce premiums.

CHAPTER 5

Medicaid, Uninsured, and the Underinsured—115 Million Problems

The Medicaid population, the uninsured, and the underinsured constitute a staggering 115 million people in the U.S. or greater than one-third of the entire population in 2006. The Medicaid population has expanded from thirty-six million in 2000 to fifty-one million in 2005, and the uninsured population has grown from 39.6 million to forty-eight million during the same period. The underinsured population was estimated at about sixteen million from a 2003 survey, with no recent comparisons. I will look at each of these groups separately and discuss the impact they have on healthcare economics.[1, 2, 3, 4]

Medicaid

Fifty-one million people were covered by Medicaid in 2005 at a cost of about $300 billion per year, with the federal government spending $177 billion and the states contributing $120 billion.[5] Unfortunately, the amount of reimbursement for hospital care is only about 90% of actual costs, leaving a shortfall of about $7 billion nationwide in 2004.[6] The reimbursement for physicians ($29 billion) was about 60% of Medicare fee schedule rates,[7] which are low to begin with and have not kept pace with inflation.

As a result of the low reimbursement schedules, access to care is more difficult for Medicaid patients. Few physicians will see these patients on a regular basis, if at all. A 2004 study found that only 62% of physicians nationwide (54% of primary care physicians and 67% of specialists) would see Medicaid patients. In many states where the fee schedules are more depressed than the Medicaid national average, the percentage of physicians accepting Medicaid patients is much lower.[8] Therefore, continuity of care with good follow-up is almost non-existent, preventive care is often meager, and the use of emergency rooms for basic medical care is the norm. The Medicaid program would be greatly improved if hospital and physician reimbursements were at least at Medicare levels. An additional $7 billion should be added to hospital payments and about $20 billion to physician compensation. This would provide some additional remuneration to providers to enable them to give the Medicaid population a more normal healthcare experience in the form of preventive care, expanded access to family physicians in their offices, reduced need to use emergency rooms for routine care, and better follow-up care for chronic illnesses. These measures would likely decrease the overall cost of care and improve the quality for this segment of the population.

Why should we care about this? Aside from the fact that we are once again allowing a large segment of our population to receive poor care because of inadequate reimbursements, we are incurring an ever-increasing tax burden. In 2000, thirty-six million people were on Medicaid, costing the government $187 billion, and in 2005 there were fifty-one million costing about $300 billion.

There are several expenses that we should focus on in an effort to reduce costs. Five percent of Medicaid patients are responsible for 50% of the expenditures.[9] These are generally patients with chronic illnesses such as asthma, heart failure, emphysema, etc. They require intensive disease management programs or at least comprehensive healthcare by adequately reimbursed physicians. These physicians need to spend the time necessary to ensure that the proper prevention measures and therapies are provided to decrease the frequency and cost of complications of these chronic problems.

Additionally, these physicians need proper reimbursement to enable them to acquire the resources and personnel to provide timely access to care in an effort to keep these patients out of the emergency rooms. This will save large sums of money in the long run.

Furthermore, since Medicaid pays for long-term nursing home care for the needy, there is a growing number of families that transfer assets from the patient to others in the family when it is anticipated that extended nursing home care will be needed. The patient then qualifies for Medicaid coverage, so the patient and family pay nothing. The annual per capita expenditure for a Medicaid patient in an institution was $57,670 in 2004 and only $4,059 for a non-institutionalized Medicaid patient. This is a fourteen times differential.[10, 11] When patients and families transfer assets or set up "Medicaid annuities" to shelter wealth, it dramatically increases governmental expenditures. Medicaid currently pays for about 50% of the total national nursing home expenditures, which includes the truly needy and those who have sheltered assets.[12] This loophole needs to be closed.

If the government were to purchase private insurance for the Medicaid population, the cost would be $3,695 per person (the average 2004 single person insurance premium) for non-institutionalized people. If we reduce the overhead of the private insurers to that of Medicare (20% vs. 1.6%), the cost of insurance would be about $3,015. The annual savings would be in excess of $1,000 per capita or about $52 billion. This figure assumes that the mode of care for the Medicaid patient would be more like that of the general population as described above. This goal is achievable with proper reimbursements to providers.

The Uninsured

Who are the uninsured? By definition, these are people who are under sixty-five years of age because people sixty-five and older are insured by Medicare. They come from all walks of life and all income levels, though most of them come from the working poor, with more than one-third earning less than $20,000 per year and about two-thirds earning less than $40,000. Over 50% are white, 30% Hispanic, and 11% black. More than two-thirds of the families have at least one full-time worker. To put their incomes into perspective, the federal poverty level for 2005 was set at an annual income of $19,350 or earnings of about $10 per hour for a family of four.[13, 14, 15, 16] The mean hourly salary in the US in 2004 was $19.14 for full-time employment,[17] and the federal minimum wage was $5.15. The uninsured are typically self-employed, work for a small company that does not offer health insurance, or are employed at a low-level job where insurance is not offered. More than 70% of the uninsured state that the high cost of either purchasing insurance directly or paying for the worker contribution is unaffordable. Other uninsured people are individuals who have lost jobs or have changed jobs and cannot afford the COBRA payments. In addition, there is a growing number of uninsured people who are illegal aliens, especially in border states. This, too, is becoming a severe problem.[18, 19]

Is it really possible that people making $10–20 per hour with a family of four cannot afford healthcare? Let's look at the average costs of employer-sponsored insurance. The average annual worker contribution toward family coverage is about $2,700. If someone gets hospitalized, the average deductible is $861. If the family members go to the doctor twice a year with a copay of $20, the cost is about $160, and if they need two prescriptions filled per month for a chronic illness, the copay could be $500 for a formulary drug.[20] The total cost would be about $4,200 per year. For a person making $10 per hour, that is about 20% of his or her total pre-tax income. Obviously, for people making $20 per hour or $40,000 per year—the national average—it is still a significant expense, but less of a stretch and should be affordable if the employer offers coverage. If the family (with an income of $40,000) had to purchase insurance separately (without an employer), the cost of the premium for family coverage would be in excess of $10,000 per year or about 25% of their pre-tax income, plus the copays and deductibles. This is not easily affordable. In most states, adults without dependents cannot qualify for Medicaid or other public health coverage.[21] Additionally, children in a low-income family may be eligible for Medicaid, but not the parents.[22] Approximately seven million children are covered under the State Children's Health Insurance Program (SCHIP), a federal/state Medicaid type of plan.[23]

Why should we care about the uninsured? In general, we are a compassionate society and do not wish anyone to experience hardship or illness. That being said, there are selfish reasons why we should care—nine hundred and twenty-two reasons to be exact. A study commissioned by Families USA, a non-profit organization, estimated that some of the costs of caring for the uninsured are translated into higher private insurance premiums. For family coverage, the additional cost is estimated at $922, and for individual premiums the cost is about $341 annually based upon 2005 data. It is estimated that about $137 billion worth of care was consumed by the uninsured in 2005. Since some of these patients were not uninsured for the entire year, about 40% was paid by public and private insurance, out-of-pocket payments accounted for 25%, and the remaining 35% ($43 billion) was uncompensated, meaning that no *direct* payment was made to the providers of the care (hospitals or physicians) through public insurance, private insurance, or out-of-pocket by patients.[24, 25, 26]

Money is allocated to hospitals to partially pay for indigent/uninsured patients through the Medicare and Medicaid programs *indirectly* by paying for interns and residents. Additionally, some states give hospitals "charity care" payments to offset, at least partially, hospital uncollected costs for certain patients who qualify based upon low income as evidenced on their tax returns. This total assistance amounted to about $14 billion in 2005.[27, 28] The remaining uncompensated hospital costs are partially paid by the private insurers as a result of hospitals being able to negotiate higher rates of reimbursement to allow them to recover some of their losses. This phenomenon is known as "cost shifting". In 2004, the American Hospital Association estimated that private insurers paid about 130% of actual hospital costs for their subscribers while Medicare and Medicaid paid about 90% of the costs for theirs.[29] It was estimated that a total of $29 billion was paid by private insurers to offset the uncompensated expenses (predominantly to hospitals) of the uninsured in 2005. This excess compensation was shifted to all of us purchasing insurance and resulted in increased premiums of $341 for individuals and $922 for families.[30]

Sources of payments for the uninsured 2005	$Billions	Sources of payments for *uncompensated* care	$Billions
Public/private insurance	49	Federal and state "charity" payments	14
Out-of-pocket	31	Private insurance "payments"	29
Uncompensated	43	Total	43
Indigent clinics	7		
Total payments	130		
Expenses never reimbursed			
Physician services	7		
Total health costs of the uninsured	137		

State and local governments also pay for indigent clinics at a cost in excess of $7 billion annually. A small amount of private funding for indigent clinics in the amount of $200 million also exists.[31]

The amount of uncompensated care attributed to physicians was about $5 billion in 2001[32] and was estimated to be $7.1 billion in 2004. These losses are normally not recouped, as they are with hospitals. Medicare and Medicaid do not take into account the physician portion of uncompensated care in their reimbursements. Since physicians are generally not in practices large enough to negotiate with private payers, they likewise do not receive enhanced compensation for the uninsured from that source either.

Another reason we should care about the uninsured is that they are part of the work force of the country. Without routine and preventive healthcare, they are subject to increased health risks, thereby producing more absenteeism and lost productivity. This costs businesses and our society, as a whole, huge amounts of money.

Additionally, children suffer from a lack of preventive medical care, vaccinations, and treatment for pediatric illnesses. Without proper attention, these problems can lead to learning disabilities, permanent injuries, frequent hospitalizations, and a future significant financial burden on society, as well as a shortened life expectancy and lost productivity.

A more compelling reason is that any one of us can become uninsured through no fault of our own. You might change jobs and find that the new position does not give you insurance until a three-month probation period ends. You decide that the cost of COBRA is too expensive, so you choose not to buy coverage. You are forty-five years old and about two months into your new job. Suddenly, you have a large heart attack or are in a serious car accident that ends up costing you about $200,000 in hospital and physician bills. Not only do you have these bills to pay that could cause you to declare bankruptcy or put a serious financial strain on you and your family, but you also have a medical condition that may make it difficult for you to obtain health insurance at a reasonable price, if at all.

Furthermore, over half of the uninsured households report someone who has skipped a medical treatment, avoided filling a prescription, or cut the frequency of taking medications during the past year.[33] Uninsured adults are four times more likely than insured adults to forego preventive care. Eighteen thousand deaths per year in the non-elderly population can be attributed to being uninsured. The non-elderly uninsured are also three times more likely to die in the hospital than insured patients because they are sicker, with more advanced diseases, when they finally come to the hospital.[34]

In 2001, the per capita spending on the uninsured was about $1,587, and the per capita spending for all non-elderly people was about $2,233.[35] The difference between these two amounts is about $646. If we multiply this by the 45 million uninsured in 2004 and increase the amount by about 39%, which is the increase in personal health expenditures from 2001 to 2004, we come up with $40 billion. This is the additional amount of money necessary to provide healthcare to the uninsured. Hold on to this number. We will use it later.

The Underinsured

This group of people in the U.S. is made up of individuals and families who are insured all year but are without adequate financial protection when faced with high out-of-pocket expenses relative to incomes. In general, this group has medical expenses greater than or equal to 10% of income or 5% for low-income people below 200% of the poverty level[36] or healthcare expense deductibles greater than or equal to 5% of income.[37] A 2005 study found that about sixteen million Americans are underinsured. The causes of this problem are related to: a) high deductibles and copays; b) increased patient cost-sharing of premiums; and c) restricted benefits. All of these are designed to keep the overall cost of health insurance premiums offered by employers lower than they would otherwise be. This effort to keep premiums under control often shifts the financial burden to the employees, some of whom cannot afford it.

We see this in our practice when we are faced with annual increases in premiums of 10–27%. We are, therefore, forced to purchase insurance products for ourselves and our staff that have higher annual deductibles and increased copays for hospitalizations, doctor visits, and medications. We have tried to refrain from increasing the amounts that the employees pay as part of their contribution so that everyone can afford the insurance. It becomes a trade-off between higher monthly premiums and higher out-of-pocket costs for care. We feel that at least we are providing comprehensive coverage with some out-of-pocket risk, but the catastrophic coverage is intact. A global consequence of this type of "cost containment", especially for lower-income people, is generally some reduction in the use of the benefit so as to avoid the escalating out-of-pocket costs. The 2005 survey found that about one-third to one-half of the underinsured missed filling a prescription, skipped a test or doctor visit, did not see a specialist for a medical problem, changed their way of life to pay medical bills, and felt they would have had better medical care if they had had a better insurance plan.[38]

Applying the same analysis from the uninsured section regarding the potential out-of-pocket costs per year of about $4,200, we find that a family earning $20,000 could not afford to pay for this coverage. That family would look to insurance for catastrophic care only. Clearly, people have to make choices regarding paying for essentials in their lives and using the money for more discretionary purposes; the lower-income working people, however, do not have the leeway to make these choices, especially when they have one or more chronic illnesses such as diabetes, heart disease, emphysema, cancer, etc. Their choices are between food, rent, and medical bills.

Nine percent of people with incomes greater than $35,000 are underinsured, and 3% have incomes greater than $60,000.[39] Their choices are more discretionary and may be between a new car, a vacation, or some other luxury item as described in the chapter on physicians.

So, again, why should we all care about this? With healthcare costs increasing and insurance premiums increasing faster than the actual costs, any one of us can be underinsured at any time depending upon our income level and misfortune. Furthermore, we are again faced with a part of our workforce that is not receiving comprehensive care and will likely have more absenteeism, reduced productivity, and less satisfaction in the workplace.

I see a growing number of patients daily who cannot afford their deductibles and/or their costs of medications as a consequence of employers trying to keep health insurance premiums from increasing. I am providing more sample medications than ever before to patients who cannot afford to purchase them, and it seems like this number is increasing every month. I believe the sixteen million people designated as underinsured is an underestimate and is likely far higher.

Bottom Line:

- There are substantial costs to our society for having about 115 million people (one-third of the population) without comprehensive healthcare coverage. These include lost productivity, higher health costs since they do not receive adequate preventive care, lack of adequate pediatric care, misuse of emergency rooms at very high cost, increased tax burden, and premature death.

- Any of us can become underinsured or uninsured depending upon our work environment and income level. We would then be subject to the stress of a major illness and the uncertainty of how to pay for it.

- Medicaid expenditures are growing rapidly despite federal and state efforts to reduce the eligibility and scope of coverage. From 2000 to 2004, the rate of annual growth was between 7.4% and 12.9%.

- The total uncompensated cost (not paid directly to providers) of delivering healthcare to the uninsured is about $50 billion per year.

- The Medicaid program, as it stands today, provides poor care to its recipients and costs the government more than it should. The $50 billion savings in the Medicaid program, by providing a more traditional type of health coverage, could pay for all of the *uncompensated* costs of the uninsured.

Expenditures for Medicaid and Uninsured (100M people):	$Billions
Medicaid	300
Uninsured	
Public/private insurance	49
out of pocket	31
"Excess" private insurance payments	29
Indirect govt/charity payments	14
Indigent clinics	7
Uncompensated physician expenses	7
Total actual expenditure	437

Cost to provide standard health insurance for 100 M people:	
Individual average insurance premium 2004 @$3,695	370
Individual average insurance premium with Medicare overhead 2004 @$3,015	300
Medicaid nursing home payments (1.3 m people @ $60,000)	78
Total costs with Medicare overhead	378
Total savings (total actual expenditure - total costs)	59

This chart demonstrates that providing "private" health insurance to the Medicaid and the uninsured populations will save about $59 billion annually and give them the benefit of having comprehensive healthcare in a traditional setting.

- Private insurance premiums are estimated to be increased by an average of $341 for individual coverage and $922 for family coverage, for a total of $29 billion, as a result of providers (predominantly hospitals) trying to recoup their losses from uncompensated care by negotiating higher reimbursement rates.

- As more people are dropped from the safety net of Medicaid in a cost containment effort, they are added to the ranks of the uninsured. This puts more pressure on hospitals and physicians to provide "uncompensated" care. As a result, the savings generated in the Medicaid program are merely shifted to indirect governmental (federal, state, and local) payments to hospitals, resulting in higher taxes as well as higher private insurance premiums. There are no net savings.

- It is true that we have *universal healthcare* in that anyone who needs care can come to any emergency room and be treated, whether or not he or she has insurance. We do not, however, have *universal health coverage*, which would provide reimbursement for care in more reasonable, cost-effective settings, such as private physician offices, and also cover appropriate hospital expenses. This would provide preventive care, improve the health status of this segment of the population, save money, and keep the costs at a more reasonable level.

CHAPTER 6

Pharmaceutical Companies— A Global Challenge

Pharmaceutical companies have come up with some truly remarkable discoveries in all fields of medicine over the past sixty years that have saved lives and significantly reduced suffering for hundreds of millions of people worldwide. This does not happen on the cheap, however. The cost of bringing a chemical to market can be in excess of $800 million, takes an average of about fifteen years, and only one in ten thousand chemicals is successful.[1] Although I am not advocating bringing out the violin to express my concern for the well-being of these companies, we need to accept the fact that developing a new drug and bringing it to market is a costly endeavor that requires years of basic chemical research, animal testing, and ultimately large studies involving patients to prove safety and efficacy.

The U.S. healthcare system consumes a huge amount of medications annually in the inpatient and outpatient setting. As we all know, many of us are taking numerous medications each day for various chronic medical conditions at a cost that is growing more unaffordable monthly. Many senior citizens, the uninsured, and the underinsured are forced to choose between food and drugs constantly. I see this every day in my practice and try my best to consolidate medications and provide patients with samples whenever possible.

This chapter will analyze the industry and show where the costs are, how they compare to other countries (in particular Canada), and what can realistically be done to bring the costs down to a more manageable level. In an effort to discuss the economics of the industry, I will uncover some interesting expense and profit statistics, involving the largest companies, to show where a large part of your money goes when you purchase medications.

The Basics

Drug companies are often multinational entities with headquarters in many of the industrialized countries of the world. These are huge operations that coordinate research, manufacturing, distribution, and marketing of pharmaceutical agents globally. A patented drug is one that is protected from being manufactured as a generic for many years after the chemical is *discovered*. Once the patent runs out, the drug can be produced by any other company. At that time, it is usually sold as a generic at a markedly reduced price compared to the patented drug price.

This protection allows the company that spent the time and money discovering the chemical and bringing it to market to earn substantial profits to offset those expenses. In the U.S. alone, there are dozens of such companies.

A recent study of the seven largest pharmaceutical companies in the U.S. demonstrated that they had combined revenues of $193 billion in 2004.[2] Of this amount, they spent 32% on marketing, advertising, and administration; earned 18% as profit; and spent only 14% on research and development (R and D). Overall, for the past ten years, drug companies have reported three to five times the profit margin of the median amount for all the Fortune 500 companies.[3] Total marketing expenses were about 1.5 times that of R and D, and profit was about 30% higher than R and D. The industry as a whole spent almost $28 billion in 2004 for marketing.[4] With profit margins so high compared to other large corporations and the need for newer drugs to treat diseases, such as Alzheimer's, diabetes, cystic fibrosis, cancer, arthritis, and many others, it would perhaps have been nice to see R and D higher than the other two items, but, alas, it is capitalism. Another huge expense for these companies has been CEO salaries, which came to about $92 million with an average of $13 million per person without stock options. The top thirty-six executives earned a total of $188 million, with stock options amounting to an additional $296 million.[5] A tidy sum. Could some of this money have been used to lower the cost of drugs and to fund research?

International Comparisons

Let's now turn to the reasons our prices for drugs are higher than those of any other country.

Prices for drugs in most industrialized countries are about 50–60% of those in the U.S.[6,7] There are several mechanisms by which these countries have managed to keep prices very low. The overriding theme is that each country negotiates the purchasing price for each drug with each pharmaceutical company and can establish comparatively lower pricing as a consequence of being able to bargain on behalf of its entire population. This creates pricing well below market values. Contrast that with the U.S., where each hospital, drugstore, or chain and insurance company, representing a much smaller number of people, has to negotiate with the pharmaceutical companies for pricing. For example, Canada bargains on the basis of a population of thirty-one million people, whereas a U.S. hospital bargains on the basis of perhaps ten thousand admissions per year. Which do you think will have better negotiating power? The country has complete market power, so if the drug company wants to sell a particular drug in that country, it needs to come to terms with the country's negotiating board. Once the price is set, it then becomes illegal to sell the drug at any higher price.

More specifically, countries other than the U.S. use one or more of the following strategies:[8]

- Reference pricing—compares prices of specific drugs with other countries and refuses to pay more than the mean price.
- Therapeutic class pricing—limits pricing to the average or lowest price of other drugs in that particular class of drugs, such as beta blockers, anti-inflammatory agents, etc., regardless of how much "more effective" the new agent may be.
- Volume controls—limits quantity of specific drugs per year.
- Profit controls—limits profits on drugs with an excess profits tax.
- Marketing approvals—countries require lengthy permit applications and cost effectiveness studies, which can take many months to accom-

plish, thereby delaying the appearance of new, costly patented drugs on the market. It is generally known that low pricing may expedite the process.

- Restrictive formularies—specific lists of drugs available for use.
- Prescribing guidelines—physicians must follow specific guidelines in order to use medications.
- Prescribing budgets—limits on the amount of money spent on drugs and incentives to physicians for withholding costly drug therapy.
- Reduced promotions—marked limitations on the amount and type of advertising and drug promotions to physicians and direct-to-the-public advertising.

Another clever mechanism by which most other countries control drug costs is through the use of parallel trade. This is defined as "the legal movement of identical products between nation states without the explicit consent of the original manufacturer".[9] In essence, if a U.S. manufacturer sells drug A to Italy for $1 a pill and to Spain for $1.50, Italy can sell the same drug to Spain for $1.25, make a profit, and still undercut the deal made between Spain and the U.S. manufacturer. Italy also does not need the permission of the producer of the pill to sell it to Spain. Therefore, countries unable to extract low pricing from a specific manufacturer can still obtain a relatively low price by purchasing it from some other country. This trade policy drives down pricing from the manufacturer since it knows that any country can sell to any other country, thereby creating an additional element for buyer-side leverage. In a 2003 study, five selected European countries saved a total of €631 million on parallel trade alone.[10] Also, the prices paid by the various industrialized countries are common knowledge among each other, so the ability to bargain with "inside information" is easy.

One simple example of Canadian drug pricing advantage over the U.S. is for the new drug Paxil CR. The 12.5 mg tablet in Canada has a negotiated price of $1.5861 Canadian, which is about $1.25 in U.S. dollars. The manufacturer, GlaxoSmithKline, made a payment to the Canadian government of $310,403.64 in March 2005 to offset "excess revenues" generated by charging prices higher than allowed by Canadian law.[11] That same pill can be purchased for $1.89 to $2.33 (U.S. dollars) from several online Canadian drugstores. By comparison, U.S. online pharmacies will sell the same tablet for $2.20 to $3.29.[12] The median online price for Canada is $2, and for the U.S. it is $2.80. This is but one of thousands of examples of the price differential between Canada and the U.S.

Aside from other countries benefiting from price controls to keep the unit cost of drugs lower than free market values, the aggregate loss of revenue to the drug companies causes several other consequences not necessarily stated, but easily inferred. It is estimated that the total amount of lost revenue to the pharmaceutical companies from just the OECD member countries was about $18 billion to $27 billion in 2003.[13] In other words, if there were no price controls in these countries, the income to the pharmaceutical companies would have been that much higher. One could argue that this huge amount of money could have been spent on the development of perhaps twenty new drugs annually. This could lead to cures for or the reduction of suffering from many diseases for tens of millions of people worldwide. Alternatively, the companies could have used this money globally to reduce the cost of drugs to all of us or could have kept the money for additional profit. Americans, by paying higher prices for their drugs, are supporting the R and D efforts of the pharmaceutical companies to a much greater extent than any other country on an absolute and a relative basis! The rest of the world should at least say "Thank you".

Ever-Increasing Costs

Why is the total cost of medications in the U.S. increasing so rapidly?

There are two aspects to increased costs. First is the cost per unit of drug or the cost per pill or injection. As was described above, other countries will limit the annual increases in unit pricing based upon some benchmark, such as the cost of living in each country. It is common for drug companies *not* to increase prices annually in these countries in order to remain competitive since pricing will be influenced by parallel trade, as described above. In the U.S., however, it is very common to see annual price increases for brand-name drugs that significantly exceed the cost of living. The AARP reported an overall 6% price increase for drugs in 2005, compared to a 3.4% rise in inflation. Some drugs increased much more. Ambien was up 19.5%, several inhalers for asthma were up 18–22%, and Lantus insulin was up 15%. From 2000 to 2005, the average drug price increase estimated by the AARP was 5.8% per year, and the rate of inflation was 2.7%. Therefore, drug pricing increased more than twice as fast as the cost of living.[14] This has occurred despite huge profits and large senior management salaries.

The second component of the total increased cost of prescription medications is the number of units (pills, injections, etc.) purchased. From 1994 to 2005, the number of prescriptions purchased in the U.S. increased 71% from 2.1 to 3.6 billion. The U.S. population grew about 9%, and the number of prescriptions per person grew from 7.9 to 12.3 per year, a 55% increase.[15] Why was there such a large growth in the number of drugs used per person? Looking at cardiology again as a benchmark, there are many chronic conditions that research has demonstrated will improve or stabilize with additional medication. This allows patients to live longer and have a better quality of life. For example, let's look at chronic heart failure, the most common cause of hospitalization in this country. Not long ago, there were only two or three drugs that were used to treat this condition (a diuretic, digoxin, and a potassium supplement). Now we use a combination of up to ten drugs (a beta blocker like Coreg, a diuretic, digoxin, potassium, spironolactone, an ACE inhibitor like Vasotec, an ACE blocker like Diovan, aspirin, a statin for coronary artery disease, and, sometimes, another diuretic and warfarin). For chronic coronary artery disease, the number of medications has also significantly increased from using aspirin and a beta blocker like Lopressor to adding an ACE inhibitor and/or an ACE blocker, a statin, Plavix, calcium blocker, warfarin, and a chronic nitrate. All of these additions are the result of studies and then guidelines for appropriate care. I have many patients who take more than twenty pills daily for a combination of chronic illnesses. Most of them are doing well and are able to lead productive lives, generally free from hospitalizations. The cost of taking all these drugs is huge if they have a prescription plan and prohibitive without some type of insurance. I have no doubt that some, if not many, of my patients do not take all the drugs as prescribed as a result of financial issues or just not having enough time in the day to fit all this in!

The number of drugs—and in many instances the dosages that we will use in the future—will only increase as more research indicates benefit. As hard as it may be to believe, many studies have indicated that there is a serious underutilization of medications, especially in cardiology.[16, 17, 18, 19, 20] A December 2004 study demonstrated that there were 1.2 million

Americans not receiving anticoagulation for a rhythm problem called atrial fibrillation. The absence of this drug leads to higher incidences of stroke. Other studies have documented serious underutilization of appropriate medications in the ranges of 50–75% deficiencies.[21] Physician educational programs have been underway nationwide to eliminate these shortfalls and to be sure patients are given the correct therapies.[22] The good news is that these programs have been successful, and the bad news is that the number of medications being prescribed is growing enormously. Between 2000 and 2004, taking into account the increased cost per pill and the increased number of pills, the overall national expenditure for drugs increased an average of 12.5% per year. This is about three to four times the rate of inflation.[23]

Bringing Prices Down

What can we do to make the cost of pharmaceuticals more affordable in the U.S.? If we accept the fact that drugs will be used in greater numbers and the doses will likely increase as well, there is no real hope in reducing the demand for these chemicals. The only way to improve pricing, in a free market economy, is to enable Americans to negotiate with the drug companies using a larger population base and/or to allow Americans to purchase drugs internationally, as other countries do. We could allow Medicare to bargain for its forty-five million patients and get substantial discounts. The number of people covered by Medicare is greater than the entire population of Canada. Therefore, Medicare patients should be able to obtain similar pricing. Other consortia should be allowed to form to give greater market power to the purchaser, such as all Blue Cross and Blue Shield companies together. States could form purchasing groups of private insurers that will allow greater leverage. Also, we should, as a country, be able to engage in parallel trade, which will also reduce costs. This is currently illegal. If the U.S. got into the game and began to ratchet down prices, the pharmaceutical industry worldwide would perhaps be forced to reduce its profits or senior management compensation or increase pricing to other countries to make up the losses. The world would more evenly share the burden of funding research.

Since the U.S. economy is based upon capitalism, we have not permitted the government to set price controls for these products as other countries have. Additionally, and probably more importantly, the drug industry in the U.S. has a great deal of power. It will continue to lobby against these measures and will likely continue to be successful. It will take some brave souls in Congress and the White House to force change and do what is necessary. The pain of not being able to afford necessary medications is becoming unbearable to all of us. I see this in my office practice every day when patients tell me their pharmaceutical expenses put them in a position where they must choose between eating, paying rent, or purchasing their drugs. We should not be unduly influenced by the drug industry when it tries to scare us into believing that lower pricing will mean less spent on R and D and that the next wonder drug will not be there when we need it. As shown in this chapter, there is plenty of money to go around now and even more when the other countries of the world pay their fair share.

CHAPTER 7

Other Considerations

There are other causes of the high cost of healthcare in the U.S., and it is beneficial to analyze them to see just how significant they are and to what extent changes can be made to reduce expenses.

Medical Malpractice

The malpractice tort system in this country has gotten a great deal of press in the past several years, with malpractice premiums increasing at alarming rates and premiums at extremely high levels. In many states, certain specialties are seeing significant losses of physicians, making access to these types of care very difficult and, as a result, delays of care can be dangerous to patients. We have had several instances where no neurosurgeon, gastroenterologist, or neurologist was on staff at one or more of our hospitals.

Neurosurgery and obstetrics-gynecology are suffering from extraordinary premiums. In some parts of the country, an obstetrician-gynecologist (OB-GYN) can pay about $300,000 per year and an internist $65,000. In Pennsylvania, the premium for a general surgeon was $33,684 in 2000 and $72,518 in 2003. In addition, there is a required (mandated) contribution to the state secondary insurance fund of 43% of the premium or about $31,180 for a total of about $104,000. In an effort to be even-handed, when statistics like these are cited, it is hard to know how many lawsuits these physicians have had, what the outcomes were, whether they are good doctors, or whether they are practicing recklessly. It is possible that some of these premiums are justified, but certainly the Pennsylvania increases are extreme. My malpractice premiums have increased by about 25–50% per year for the past four years without any claims being brought against me. There is no doubt that premiums have increased rapidly and that costs are getting out of hand.[1] Additionally, a large number of physicians have given up certain types of practice as a result of litigation concerns, such as reading mammography by radiologists. There are OB-GYNs who now just do gynecology, and some of them have limited their practices to office gynecology, eliminating surgery. Have you ever wondered why it sometimes takes so long to get an appointment to see a gynecologist or to get a mammogram? The reason is that there are fewer of these physicians, in part as a result of litigation concerns.

How does the malpractice environment in the U.S. compare to other countries and could it be a reason for the higher healthcare spending that we face? A 2005 study compared the U.S., Canada, United Kingdom, and Australia, all of which have similar tort systems. The number of malpractice claims in the U.S. per one thousand people was 50% higher than in the U.K. and Australia and 450% higher than in Canada. Additionally, the average awards from litigation per capita were in similar ratios.[2] These figures would attest to the more litigious nature of our society and could explain some of the increased costs.

I do not want to get into the whole malpractice debate, however, except to discuss the impact on healthcare costs. There are direct and indirect causes of the increased cost of healthcare as a result of malpractice issues. The direct sources of expense are the high and growing malpractice premiums. This cost is factored into the reimbursement rates that Medicare pays to physicians and hospitals. To the extent that most private insurers use Medicare as their benchmark, it can affect their reimbursement schedules as well. The increases in compensation have not at all kept pace with the rising malpractice premiums, but there is some minimal additional compensation periodically added to the amount given to physicians in the reimbursement schedules.

Tort reform would likely slow the rate of malpractice premium increases. In some states, premiums have actually decreased. Admittedly, the total savings for the national healthcare expenditures would be very small but welcomed by physicians and hospitals. Some of the savings would be passed on to the consumer by slower increases in health insurance premiums, but this would be relatively inconsequential.

The other element is the indirect costs associated with the threat of malpractice litigation. The Physician Insurers Association of America (PIAA) has stated that "failure to diagnose" an illness is the most common cause of filing a lawsuit.[3] As a result, it is easy to understand why physicians order so many tests. The simple fact is that, in many instances, we order an extra X-ray, blood test, MRI, etc. to be sure that we are not missing something, especially when the risk is of high consequence to the health of the patient. We would never knowingly put a patient in danger by ordering extra studies, but the additional testing is like wearing a belt and suspenders.

I am confronted with this every day when I am asked to see a person in the emergency room with chest pain, for instance. Many times, I will keep the patient in the hospital overnight to "rule out" a heart attack even though I believe the patient's history and preliminary tests do not necessarily indicate that the symptoms are from a cardiac origin. We are relying on the patient to give us an accurate history of his pain and other symptoms. Often the patients are not particularly insightful or articulate, making the gathering of this information difficult and often inaccurate. Hence, they get admitted. If they do not, I will often perform a stress test before discharging them from the ER after a whole host of tests were ordered by the ER physician—once again, to be sure I am not missing an atypical presentation of a heart problem. This is costly and time-consuming and is repeated thousands of times a day all over the country. But: "It is better to be safe than sorry." Many of these patients could realistically be sent home without much of this workup. On the other hand, if you make a mistake in the diagnosis and send someone home who should have stayed and he goes on to have a heart attack and dies, it is both a tragedy and a major malpractice event.

In other instances, radiologists equivocate on X-ray reports and suggest additional studies. A shadow on a chest X-ray that may or may not be significant is reported with a disclaimer and a suggestion for a CAT scan of the chest to be sure it is not cancer. As a non-radiologist, I am not in a position to say that the CAT scan is unwarranted, and therefore the additional study is usually performed. Failure to diagnose breast cancer on mammography has been a leading cause of malpractice suits against radiologists. Is it any wonder that the frequency of reporting abnormalities on mammograms can be two to five times as common in the U.S. as compared to other countries?[4] This leads to more frequent breast biopsies with a high likelihood of a negative result. And so on and so on! This all costs money, and when duplicated nationwide in every specialty every day, it costs big money.

This type of behavior is called "defensive medicine" and is practiced daily, multiple times per day, and by virtually all physicians. An extensive governmental study performed by the Office of Technology Assessment (OTA) in 1994 defined defensive medicine as follows:

> Defensive medicine occurs when doctors order tests, procedures, or visits, or avoid high-risk patients or procedures, primarily (but not necessarily solely) to reduce their exposure to malpractice liability. When physicians do extra tests or procedures primarily to reduce malpractice liability, they are practicing positive defensive medicine. When they avoid certain patients or procedures, they are practicing negative defensive medicine. Under this definition, a medical practice is defensive even if it is done for other reasons (such as belief in a procedure effectiveness, desire to reduce medical uncertainty, or financial incentives), provided that the primary motive is to avoid malpractice risk. Also, the motive need not be conscious. Over time some medical practices may become so ingrained in customary practice that physicians are unaware that liability concerns originally motivated their use. Most importantly, defensive medicine is not always bad for patients. Although political or media references to defensive medicine almost always imply unnecessary and costly procedures, OTA's definition does not exclude practices that may benefit patients. Rather, OTA concluded that a high percentage of defensive medical procedures are ordered to minimize the risk of being wrong when the medical consequences of being wrong are severe.[5]

The OTA estimated that the cost of defensive medicine was no greater than 8% of diagnostic procedures. I believe you can add to this some elements of therapy as well, since treating some illnesses in certain ways is also likely defensive. An example is the use of antibiotics in some instances. How often have you gone to your doctor with a viral illness, like a cold or a sore throat, and walked out of his office with an antibiotic? Some of this prescribing is to pacify you and some because of a lingering uncertainty of the diagnosis. It could be "strep throat", and doctors need to "cover themselves" so that they can lessen the risk of a complication. Is this bad medical practice or just being careful?

A 2005 survey of physicians regarding their practice patterns revealed that 59% *often* ordered more tests than were medically indicated, usually imaging such as X-rays, CAT scans, MRIs, etc. Thirty-three percent prescribed more drugs, and 32% ordered invasive procedures to confirm a diagnosis, such as breast biopsies for breast cancer, "just to be sure". Fifty-two percent *often* referred patients to specialists beyond true medical necessity to be extra careful from a malpractice standpoint. For example, an elderly patient, or even a younger person with several medical problems, seldom goes to the operating room without a preoperative consultation by an internist or cardiologist. This has virtually become the standard of care. Some of this is just good medical care, and some is "defensive medicine" being practiced by the surgeon and anesthesiologist. A total of 93% of the survey physicians reported that they "sometimes" or "often" engaged in some type of defensive medicine.[6]

Therefore, in order to determine the overall costs, it might be reasonable to apply the 8% to hospital care, outpatient testing, and prescription drug costs. This yields an expenditure of about $87 billion per year when using 2004 total national expenditures. This may not be such a far-fetched number since, as indicated above, not all defensive medicine is a conscious act and much of it has likely been incorporated into practice guidelines and protocols that we are urged to follow by the government and specialty societies like the American College of Cardiology, American College of Radiology, and others.

Not much in the way of savings was anticipated by the OTA study as a consequence of tort reform. I believe this is correct. Physicians have become very risk averse in the past twenty or so years, and many of these concerns have been translated into conservative patient management protocols. Patient safety and "failure to diagnose" have taken on a life of their own; there is no going back. I reluctantly agree with many critics that tort reform, though necessary, will not substantially reduce the cost of healthcare in the foreseeable future.

Equally informative is the fact that about one-third of physicians surveyed stated that they have avoided doing high-risk procedures and have avoided high-risk patients because of malpractice litigation threat.[7] High-risk patients were defined as those who had an unusual medical complexity and also those who had a high likelihood of litigation, such as children and patients covered by a worker's compensation claim or financial medical assistance programs.

There was a direct correlation between the frequency of "defensive medicine" activity and the real or perceived hostile malpractice environment. Tort reform could increase access to physicians for these high-risk populations.

Electronic Medical Records

There is a critical need for a centralized database that contains all the relevant information regarding a patient's health and the care he or she has received from birth to death. Why is this so important and how will it reduce costs? The care that a patient receives is fragmented and not readily available to those of us who need it relatively urgently. As a result, in many instances, tests are repeated needlessly or therapy is prescribed that could be harmful and cause injury to the patient. Delays can also occur as a result of the lack of comprehensive information, which can cause problems for the patient. For example, let's look at what happens to a patient who comes into the ER with chest pain. In most instances, patients do not know what type of existing medical problems they have, except for a very rudimentary understanding that they may or may not have heart disease. They often do not know what medications they take, what tests they had in the past, where they were performed, what the results were, or even who their doctors are. I see this every day. It could sometimes take us hours or days, with great expenditure of time and effort, to try to gather the necessary information. If the patient is urgently ill, we often cannot wait to obtain this data and must move on with our own work up, even though it may have all been performed recently.

I was asked to see a patient in the ER of one of our local hospitals, a sixty-year-old female with chest pain. Aside from telling me that her pain was severe and in the center of her chest, she was unable to give me any other useful information. I asked her pointedly if she had ever had tests for chest pain, and she said "no". Her family was so upset that they were likewise of no appreciable help. We did many tests, including EKGs, X-rays, blood tests, CAT scans, etc., all of which were negative. We admitted her to the hospital for observation and continued testing. On the second hospital day, one of her family members told me that she had been hospitalized in Philadelphia about a year ago for a similar problem but could not recall the name of the hospital. We called several hospitals and finally were able to find the one in which she was hospitalized. We then faxed an authorization signed by the patient to release to us the necessary records. They finally arrived the next day, and it turned out that she was hospitalized for the same type of pain and had undergone a cardiac catheterization, which was entirely normal. If we had access to this information in the ER via the Internet, tapping in to a centralized database, she would have likely not been admitted and would have been sent home from the ER with some antacids. This happens tens of thousands of times per day in every specialty of medicine, all over the country. Imagine the money wasted daily. It is enormous.

The adoption of electronic medical records (EMR) by practices and hospitals nationwide would eliminate this costly problem and would have many other advantages, such as increasing productivity and providing a much safer care environment by reducing errors. These systems can be designed to remind physicians to use certain drugs for certain conditions and to avoid others. They could inform us about drug interactions that should be avoided and keep track of allergies and tests that have been performed. Some of the systems could also suggest testing and therapy according to standardized protocols.

These systems would likely save money, though estimates vary. Healthcare economists have reported net savings to be about $21 billion to $77 billion per year. The cost of widespread connectivity is approximately $2.5 billion. These systems are not inexpensive, and the cost of deployment is about $28 billion per year for the first ten years, by some estimates.[8, 9] Currently, the expenses are being borne by the providers (doctors and hospitals). This is quite different from *all* other countries that have these systems where the expense is covered by the government and/or the health insurers who stand to benefit from the programs. Furthermore, the U.S. government has allocated minimal money to the endeavor. A 2006 bill would establish funding at about $150 million per year for four years, even though the estimated capital cost is about $156 billion over five years plus $48 billion to operate the national network.[10] I see another unfunded mandate coming down the tracks. Community and Regional Health Information Organizations (RHIO), funded by state governments and various insurance companies, are springing up in various parts of the country in an effort to provide easy sharing of patient records.[11] Even if the savings are modest, the improved safety that these systems provide is immeasurable. There needs to be a greater national commitment to this endeavor in terms of standardization and money. The process has begun, but it requires a much more robust effort.

The Cost of Chronic Illnesses

It is intuitively obvious that a large disparity exists between expenditures on those of us who are chronically ill and those who are not. The healthiest 50% of our population accounts for only 3.4% of total expenditures, whereas the sickest 1% is responsible for 22.3%, and the sickest 10% accounts for nearly 66%.[12] In the Medicare population, 95% of the expenses are a result of patients with two or more chronic illnesses. They make up 65% of the total number of beneficiaries. The most common chronic illnesses include heart disease, diabetes, and high blood pressure. Each is present in about 50% of the Medicare population. Translated into real dollars, the healthiest 50% among us spent $122 per person per year, and the sickest 1% was responsible for $56,000 per person per year.[13]

If we could somehow reduce the expenditures on those people with chronic illnesses by improving their health and reducing hospitalizations, we could probably save large amounts of money. I say probably because studies have not shown unequivocally that these efforts will reduce total expenses. It does sound crazy that reducing complications of illnesses and hospitalizations may not actually save money, but it is true. By providing the best care possible and extending the lives of people with diabetes, heart disease, etc., we are keeping them alive longer, and they are therefore using more lab testing, drugs, and hospital stays during their extended lifetimes. This will cost about the same, per patient, as having one or two catastrophic complications and dying prematurely.[14] I think everyone would agree that providing good care, prolonging life, improving the general state of health with less morbidity and hospital care, even if the expenses were higher, would not be a bad thing. To the extent that this might save some money over the long term, it is a real benefit. The amount of savings, however, may be minimal.

One way to achieve improved care for high-risk patients with chronic illnesses is to enroll them in "disease management" programs. These are defined as "programs that focus on one or more chronic illnesses and attempt to improve quality and reduce costs incurred by people with chronic conditions".[15] There is now an entire industry that has grown up with many companies that are in business to provide management or consultative help to insurers for these illnesses, which consume 78% of our total national healthcare expenditures.[16] These endeavors seem to be somewhat financially successful in instances where the patients are very ill and where the complications would be very costly. Examples are severe congestive heart failure, multiple complications of diabetes, and severe asthma requiring multiple hospitalizations. These are very expensive, labor-intensive programs where nurses interact with patients by telephone and/or face-to-face visits in order to make sure patients are caring for themselves correctly. The costs are usually borne by the insurance companies since they are the ones that will benefit from any savings. Therein lies the problem!

Several years ago, I had a conversation with a senior medical director of one of the major insurers in our region. We were discussing the value of these disease management programs and whether they should institute one for congestive heart failure. He was quite familiar with programs of this type and indicated that his company was not interested in initiating such a venture because the payback in savings was not assured. The reason—most patients do not stay with their, or any, insurance company for more than two years on average. The benefit of long-term disease management would accrue to the next insurer. I asked whether he would be willing to discuss this with the other two major insurance companies in our area and develop a combined program so that all the companies would benefit financially when the patients migrated from one to another. I offered to put the meeting together since I had a good relationship with the other medical directors. His response was still "no". He felt that the efforts would not be worth the potential benefits, even though he agreed that a program like this would be of great medical benefit to these high-risk patients. I received the same response from the other companies. It's all about the money!

Bottom line: Disease management programs would be of great help to improve patient compliance, well-being, and longevity, but they are not likely to save *huge* sums of money in the long run.

Medical Errors

Reduction of medical errors, particularly in the hospital setting, is a serious issue that is being addressed with new risk management programs and computerization. Estimates of savings are in the range of $5–17 billion per year.[17] This is not a great deal of money given that the total national healthcare expenditure is in excess of $1.8 trillion. Nevertheless, efforts to improve hospital safety are imperative and are being addressed.

"Excessive Use of Technology"

Much has been written over the years regarding the excessive use of technology in the U.S. compared to other countries as a cause of the higher costs for healthcare in the U.S. There is some truth to this allegation, but it is not a universal truth. Once again, data drawn from the OECD annual reports is helpful in sorting this out. Unfortunately, not every country provides information in a timely manner so that some comparisons are for different years. In a 2005 report, which amalgamates information from 2001 to 2003, the U.S. had fewer doctors, nurses, and acute hospital beds per one thousand members of the population than the median OECD country and much fewer than Canada.[18] Furthermore, the number of days per year spent in a hospital per capita was .7 for the U.S. compared to 1.0 for the median.[19] In other words, we have fewer of these resources, and, as a result of great efforts to limit hospital days, we are spending significantly less time in the hospital than most of the other industrialized countries. The fact that our spending on inpatient care is about 70% higher than the median OECD amount,[20] with salaries and drugs making up about 77% of hospital expenses, supports the notion that the increased cost is primarily a result of higher salaries and the prices of pharmaceuticals and not from over-utilization of expensive technology.

The notion that our increased costs of healthcare are driven by the acquisition of technology and other resources is likely not entirely true since we have, in general, fewer resources per capita than most other countries. It is more likely that much of the excess costs are the result of higher salaries and the price of drugs and, to some extent, defensive medicine, which causes increased utilization of some technology.

Personal Responsibility

Many Americans do not take personal responsibility for their health, resulting in significant disability leading to chronic diseases, increased need for medications and hospitalizations, and premature death.

Obesity is a huge problem for us. According to OECD data from a 2005 report, the percentage of the adult U.S. population with obesity was 31% compared to an average of 6.5% in twenty-five other countries. Canada, for instance, was about 12%. We have the highest rate of obesity in the industrialized world. From 1976–80, the percentage in the U.S. was only 15%.[21] Our eating habits are progressively worsening, and data indicates that the other countries in this survey are also experiencing significant increases in the frequency of obesity. Is it any wonder that this is occurring? Fast food, loaded with fat and carbohydrates and often "supersized", is the main staple of our diet.

I usually eat lunch in a hospital cafeteria (my usual chef salad and diet Coke). I witness relatives of my patients (who have had heart attacks, strokes, heart failure, etc.) piling trays with cheeseburgers, French fries, extra salt, Cokes, ice cream, and cake. The caloric and fat contents are huge and are direct contributors to the obesity problem. These poor dietary habits that produce obesity are also a leading cause of diabetes, coronary artery disease, high blood pressure, gall bladder disease, sleep apnea, some forms of cancer, and all of their complications. Even when patients develop these problems, they are often unable or unwilling to modify their eating habits despite numerous discussions and counseling. It is estimated that the annual national medical expenditure for obesity-related illnesses is about $75 billion.[22] It is also estimated that 27% of the growth in healthcare spending in the U.S. from 1987 to 2001, after inflation, was a consequence of obesity.[23] These figures do not include loss of productivity at work, absenteeism, and the costs associated with disability.

Smoking is another national problem that requires control. A 2005 study by the Centers for Disease Control and Prevention estimates that 21% of the adults in the U.S. smoke cigarettes.[24] Chronic illnesses associated with smoking, including secondhand smoke, are emphysema, heart disease, stroke, high blood pressure, and numerous cancers. The direct medical costs are about 7% of the total healthcare dollar or about $126 billion.[25] In addition, in 2005, the CDC estimated that the loss of productivity between 1997 and 2001 was about $92 billion annually.[26] From 1993 to 2004, the percentage of adult smokers has decreased from about 25% to 21%,[27, 28, 29] but the population in general has increased about 1% per year, thereby essentially nullifying, in total numbers, the decrease in the percentage of smokers. Canada has a similar percentage of smokers.

In my thirty-five years of professional experience, I can probably count on one hand the number of patients I have seen who have had coronary artery disease and did not smoke. The cause-and-effect relationship is incontestable. Furthermore, the vast majority of my patients who have had a major coronary event, such as a heart attack, bypass surgery or angioplasty/stent, still smoke. They will often give it up for a few weeks or months after the event as a result of being scared, but then they resume once again. It is predictable. Furthermore, almost everyone has heard the stories of how patients who have had serious lung cancer operations or have had their larynx (voice box) removed because of cancer continue to smoke, some through the holes in their necks. All true!

Substance abuse (alcohol and drugs) is a huge problem in the U.S., affecting about 1% of the population and costing $20 billion per year in direct health costs, aside from the indirect costs of lost productivity, absenteeism, drunk driving, serious accidents, disability, and loss of life.[30, 31] You may think this is a problem of the poor and inner city population, but it is hardly so. A survey from 2002 of highly educated people, all working for one company, demonstrated that 42% had used some form of illicit drugs in the past year, and 15% were assessed to have lifelong alcohol dependence.[32]

So Where Does All This Leave Us?

To sum up this chapter, there are several different types of healthcare expenditures that lead to excess costs.

First, there is the malpractice threat leading to defensive medicine and the increased use of technology. Solving this could yield about $90 billion in savings annually. This is unlikely to be accomplished any time soon, however, with a highly litigious society and a very risk-averse medical profession. On the other hand, some incremental savings could accrue from malpractice tort reform.

Second, acquisition and deployment of a national health information system could save about $20–80 billion per year, but the initial cost and time investment to put this into universal practice is huge. There does not appear to be a credible federal plan with adequate funding to accomplish this in a reasonable amount of time, but efforts are ongoing. Currently, most of the investment is being made by the providers (hospitals and physicians), which is the opposite of the rest of the industrialized world. Movement on this endeavor is in its infancy, but progress is being made and will lead to savings eventually.

Third, disease management programs for the care of chronic illnesses could be possible if the stakeholders (insurers and the state and federal governments) get behind the programs and fund them aggressively. Further impediments, however, include the lack of patient compliance toward following the relatively rigorous programs and the exorbitant cost of medications necessary to gain benefit from the programs. Some net gain can be made in this arena, but the savings are predicted to be only $17 billion annually at most and perhaps none at all. The benefits to improved survival and general well-being, however, could be enormous.

Fourth, the amount of healthcare resources per capita in the U.S. is less than both Canada and the median of the OECD. The excess costs of hospital care are overwhelmingly the result of the cost of non-physician salaries and drugs. None of these expenditures is likely to be significantly reduced. Some reduction in the use of technology could be expected if malpractice tort reform were to be enacted.

Fifth, the reduction in the number of people with "illnesses of choice", such as obesity, smoking, and substance abuse, can be a source of real savings. The total annual expenditures for these three problems are about $220 billion per year or about 12% of total healthcare costs. An approach to consider is a higher premium for people who have "illnesses of choice". Rather than charge patients a higher insurance premium for preexisting diseases such as cancer, heart attack, stroke, etc., (as is the current policy), it might be more reasonable to charge a higher premium for poor behavior. We do this in the auto insurance industry so that drivers with multiple accidents and traffic tickets are charged higher premiums. It places some of the financial burden back on the people who are using the greatest amount of financial resources. Higher premiums may cause them to assume more personal responsibility for their actions and to alter their destructive behavior.

CHAPTER 8

Stitching It Up

Us and Them

The United States is alone among the major industrialized nations of the world in that it does not mandate comprehensive healthcare insurance for all of its citizens. Canada, Japan, and the nations of the European Economic Union provide coverage for their entire populations through either taxation or mandatory contributions to "social health insurance plans". Great Britain, Ireland, Denmark, Sweden, Finland, Spain, and Portugal provide care through a system of taxation. Germany, Belgium, Luxemburg, Austria, France, and the Netherlands generally have mandatory contributions to insurance plans with some governmental payments as well. Greece and Italy have a more balanced taxation and insurance program. All citizens of other industrialized countries are covered as a result of contributions from individuals and businesses in the form of taxes or income-adjusted insurance premiums.[1] The indigent are also covered with generally the same type of plan, except that they pay no taxes or premiums. Some countries allow for the opportunity to purchase private health insurance to enhance the basic, but comprehensive, coverage.

The Canadian health system is based upon taxation on individuals and corporations. The money is transferred from the national government to the provinces and territories and is administered by them under global budgeting, which sets limits on expenditures. Hospitals and other institutions are all non-profit. All inpatient and outpatient services are covered, including physician, laboratory, and hospital fees, without any charge to the patient. In most instances, prescription drugs are also covered. All citizens are entitled to the same coverage. Private health insurance may be purchased to pay for discretionary services not covered by the province and territory health plans, such as dentistry, optometry, and some prescription drugs.

Contrast that to the U.S. In 2004, our total national healthcare expenditure was $1.8 trillion, of which 55% was financed through private funds (out-of-pocket and private insurance company payments) and 45% through public funds (Medicare, Medicaid, Department of Defense, Veterans Administration, state and local funding, and several other small categories).[2] Despite this enormous outlay of money, forty-eight million Americans are uninsured, and an additional sixteen million (probably even more) are underinsured. As discussed previously, a case can be made that the fifty-one million Medicaid patients are certainly underinsured since the poor reimbursements to hospitals and physicians often result in inadequate care. Therefore, a total of 115 million people in the U.S. (more than one-third of our population) are either uninsured or underinsured. Furthermore, this large segment of our population incurs healthcare costs in excess of $437 billion per year plus the amount paid by the underinsured. Of this $437 billion, the government pays about $346 billion (using our ever-increasing tax burden), and those with private health insurance pay an additional $29 billion in higher premiums. The remainder is paid by private insurance and out-of-pocket expenses with $7 billion of physician expense remaining uncompensated.[3] (See chart showing expenditures for Medicaid and uninsured on page 51).

To cover this entire population with private insurance, based upon the average insurance premium with Medicare overhead ($3,015),[4] the cost would be about $378 billion per year, for a savings of about $59 billion per year.

Despite the universal and comprehensive coverage of other countries, they are spending about 40% of the U.S. expenditure per person.

The Excesses

Why is our healthcare system so much more expensive than any other system in the world? There are three primary reasons.

First, our national salary structure is much wider than any other country, meaning that the difference between the average highest and average lowest salaries is greatest in the U.S., as shown in chapter two. As a consequence of this large disparity, the average physician salary is 5.5 times the average worker salary in the U.S., compared to two times in most other industrialized countries. With physician salaries so relatively high compared to other industrialized countries, other medical professionals (nurses, pharmacists, X-ray technicians, etc.) in the U.S. enjoy higher salaries than their counterparts in the rest of the industrialized world. Furthermore, healthcare professional salaries are in line with other non-healthcare professionals in the U.S. Since professional and support staff salaries constitute in excess of 50% of total national healthcare expenditures, this salary differential in the U.S. compared to other countries is a huge part of the equation.

Second, prescription drugs make up about 5% of the total cost of care, and we pay about twice the amount per drug as other countries do. We are essentially paying for the R and D of the entire world. Additionally, high cost devices, such as pacemakers, defibrillators, prosthetic joints, etc., share similar pricing, adding to the excess expenses.

Third, the cost of administering the healthcare system is enormous by comparison with the situation in other countries. In 1999, we spent about 31% of national healthcare expenditures on administering the system or $1,059 per person; by comparison, Canada spent 16.7% or $307 per person. If we update these numbers and apply the same 31% to the 2004 spending total of $1.877 trillion, the amount spent on administering the

Per Capita Administrative Costs				
	1999 U.S. dollars		2004 U.S. dollars	
	U.S.	Canada	U.S.	Canada
Insurance overhead	259	47	476	86
Employers' costs to manage health benefits	57	8	105	15
Hospital administration	315	103	579	188
Nursing home administration	62	29	114	53
Administrative costs to practitioners	324	107	595	196
Home care administration	42	13	77	24
Total per capita	1059	307	1946	561

U.S. system was about $558 billion per year or $1,946 per capita. Applying Canada's percentage from 1999 to 2004 Canadian expenditures, we find that the cost was about $561 per capita.[5] If we were to adopt a Canadian-style single-payer system, our savings could be about $1,400 per person or in excess of $400 billion annually just to administer the system. Since virtually all the industrialized countries of the world have a version of a single-payer system, administrative costs in these countries are similar to Canada, thus making the U.S. unique in having a multi-layered healthcare financing system with excessive administrative costs. [6]

To attempt to explain some of the excess expenses, an article in *The New England Journal of Medicine* pointed out that in 1999 the largest private insurers in the U.S. had an average of 22.6 employees per ten thousand enrollees.[7] In Canada, however, that average was about 1.3. A single-payer system does not require underwriters or marketing departments, which can account for two-thirds of the cost of overhead in the private insurance companies. Private insurers have an overhead of about 20% compared to Medicare's overhead of only 1.8%. If private insurers had a similar overhead, there would be about $120 billion of savings annually.

Additionally, there are expenses incurred by employers to participate in our multi-payer system. These costs include benefits consultants, extra bookkeeping and accounting, and time spent analyzing multiple benefit packages and dealing with employee claims issues. Hospitals, nursing homes, home care organizations, and physicians spend enormous amounts of money for personnel who keep track of private insurers' plans, procedure codes, paper forms, patient eligibility status, claims processing, appeals for payment denials and underpayments, and for consultants to help with contract negotiations, etc. All of this would be unnecessary with a single-payer system.[8] Our practice is charged $1,100 per month by a proprietary third-party software company to process our claims so that we can submit them to most private insurers. Medicare does not have this charge since we are able to send our claims electronically *directly* to its computer system.

In simple terms, these three elements of spending (salaries, drugs, and administration) account for about 95% of the total national healthcare expenditure differences between us and Canada, as well as the remainder of the industrialized world.

Sources of Savings

With this in mind, where can we extract significant savings to bring the costs of our system in line with other industrialized countries? I will summarize the main points of the preceding chapters. This chart provides a graphic look at the categories of potential savings.

Categories	Potential Savings in Billions
Salaries (10% savings)	$90
Tort Reform/defensive medicine	$87
Information technology	$20–$80
Chronic illnesses	$17
Drugs	$62
"Illnesses of choice"	$220
M/caid, uninsured, underinsured	$60
Administration	$377

Salaries and Benefits

One approach has been to control expenditures by decreasing fee schedules for physicians or by keeping increases well below the cost of living in the Medicare program. Most private insurers mirror the Medicare fee schedule, reducing physician incomes further. The same is true for hospitals regarding government funding, with hospitals losing money on Medicare and Medicaid patients. By maintaining these low reimbursement rates for physicians and hospitals or reducing them further, we run the risk of having fewer physicians and skilled personnel. Remember that hospitals spend about 70% of their income on salaries, 7% on drugs/devices, and the remainder on relatively fixed expenses, thereby giving them little room to cut expenses. Furthermore, state governments usually dictate the patient/nurse ratios, so it would be difficult to reduce the number of professionals. In this chart, I have taken a 10% reduction in the estimated total salary costs. With the existing and anticipated shortages of nurses and physicians, supply-and-demand economics would predict that salaries cannot be dragged down without catastrophic consequences either to the number, quality, or both of skilled workers in the future. Therefore, the cutback, as shown, is unlikely to be realized without serious harm to the healthcare system. The reduction is displayed to provide evidence that these savings, even if they could be accomplished, would be relatively small compared to several other categories.

Tort Reform

The estimated expense of defensive medicine as a consequence of our litigious society is about $87 billion. Dramatically reducing defensive medicine costs by malpractice tort reform is unlikely since so many of these care patterns are heavily ingrained in nationally accepted practice protocols. Furthermore, physicians would remain very risk averse for many years even if some malpractice reforms were to occur.

Information Technology

We have begun to implement new electronic medical record computer systems in many parts of the country and in numerous areas of the healthcare system, including physicians' offices, hospitals, nursing homes, pharmacies, and outpatient testing centers. Once connected nationally, there is hope that savings of $20–$80 billion annually can be achieved. This endeavor will cost tens of billions of dollars and take many years to accomplish. We have only a rudimentary start with inadequate funding. The stakeholders (federal government and insurers) are not putting nearly enough money into the project, which is currently being financed predominantly by providers. Incremental savings will occur slowly, and patients will ultimately have a safer, more efficient system.

Chronic Illnesses

Disease management programs for chronic illnesses are not apt to diminish costs by much if at all, but they are necessary to improve the overall health of these patients. The most important savings could come from the implementation of these programs in the Medicaid and uninsured populations so that more prevention of disease and less reliance on expensive ER care can occur.

Prescription Drugs

What can be done about the cost of prescription drugs, which makes up about 10% of the total budget? We could allow Medicare with its forty-three million members to negotiate for pricing and achieve significant discounts. Other consortia of purchasers could also be established to foster improved bargaining power to reduce pricing. Additionally, we could adopt practices such as parallel trade, similar to other industrialized countries, which would allow purchasing of drugs from other countries that have already achieved pricing discounts from the drug companies. I doubt there would be much interest in allowing the U.S., as a single market of three hundred million people, to negotiate pricing with drug companies, as is typically done elsewhere. It is equally unlikely that the U.S. would institute other controls as outlined in chapter six, which would limit the access to new drugs or dictate pricing as in other industrialized countries. This type of policy would be the antithesis of capitalism. In any event, we must realize that any resultant decrease in drug company revenue would cause a reduction in profits, which could cause a decrease in R and D, executive salaries, and shareholder profits. One would hope that a responsible company would strive to maintain R and D at the expense of the other two, but this is by no means certain since these for-profit companies are very mindful of the need to produce profits for their shareholders and to take care of the senior executives. There can also be a discussion among all the world's industrialized nations to try to achieve an understanding regarding the need for a balance between low pricing, company profit, and a healthy R and D budget by allowing for higher pricing in their countries so that our prices could decrease. This is likewise improbable since each of the other countries is having its own healthcare expenditure crises, and I doubt there would be any sympathy for our plight or that of the drug companies. Sixty-two billion dollars represents a one-third reduction in costs, accounting for the difference between our unit costs and those in Canada.

"Illnesses of Choice"

Obesity, smoking, and substance abuse account for about $220 billion of medical care per year. Attempts have been made to reduce these health problems, but so far there's been little success. We should consider increasing health insurance premiums for those who have these problems to reduce some of the financial burden on the system and to incentivize improved behavior. Taking personal responsibility for unhealthy behavior is reasonable and fair. Automobile insurance premiums are increased for people with poor driving records.

Medicaid, Uninsured, and Underinsured

The total expenditure for healthcare to cover these three groups (115 million people or more than one-third of the U.S. population) was about $437 billion in 2004. This comes to approximately $3,767 per person. As indicated above, the savings could be about $60 billion per year by insuring these patients with a single-payer, Medicare-type insurance product with a very low overhead. This will likely yield improved healthcare for these patients as well. Remember that Medicare's operating costs are about 1.8% compared to the average private insurer of about 20%.

Administrative Costs

The final area of potential savings is from the administrative costs of the healthcare industrial complex. As demonstrated, the savings from converting to a single-payer system similar to Canada can be huge, with about $400 billion ($1,400 per person) at stake. This is by far the largest amount of money that can be saved by changing the parameters of our system.

Single Payer vs. the Existing System

There are many proposals that are considered a single-payer system. They generally come across as and are criticized for sounding like socialized medicine. An example is one published in August 2003 by the Physicians' Working Group.[9] They typically advocate one governmental payer, dissolution of the private insurance companies, and the adoption of regional and/or national spending budgets, much like the Canadian system. Critics have railed against these proposals, fearing lack of patient choice of doctors and hospitals, reduction in benefits and scope of care as a result of budgetary constraints, disruption of the free market dynamics of the private health system, elimination of the private insurance companies, global budgets that might produce long waiting times to see physicians and have testing or treatments as in Canada and the U.K., loss of entrepreneurial energy, and placement of too much control in the hands of the government.

On the other hand, one can adopt a system such as Medicare for the entire population. I think most people would agree that Medicare is a great program that has given seniors wonderful medical care, and it is *not* socialized medicine. The senior patients have freedom of choice with regard to physician and hospital use. All necessary services are covered as a result of panels of experts who decide about the reasonableness of treatments. Access to care is prompt in most cases, and there is still an entrepreneurial philosophy among providers to offer a good service package to entice patients to stay with each physician or hospital.

One negative aspect of the Medicare system is the absolute control over fees for service to physicians, hospitals, and other providers. The federal government manipulates these fee schedules to induce usage behavior, in order to achieve spending goals that it believes are in the best interests of the country, as opposed to allowing the free market to decide. An example is the decreasing of hospital payments for certain high-tech procedures such as coronary stenting and angioplasty, which reduces their use. Fees to specialists have been decreased, and those to family physicians have been increased to induce more physicians to practice family medicine. Another example is the reduction in all physician reimbursements in an attempt to reduce overall costs. A further issue of distress with Medicare is the rising patient cost of the system with increasing out-of-pocket expenditures that are especially difficult for low-income seniors. In general, however, the system works well and provides excellent care for the elderly. The same system can be used by the entire population with huge savings as a result of lower overhead compared to the existing multi-payer system.

The major problem we are having with the existing arrangement of private insurance coverage, on the other hand, is the cost of redundancy and the layering of the administrative aspects of the system. Each of the several hundred companies has its own computer system, billing system, codes, buildings, executives, medical directors, computer engineers, data processing personnel, consultants, advertising, lawyers, accountants, underwriters, utilization nurses, administrative personnel, and profits all costing in excess of ten times the administrative overhead of Medicare. On the consumer side, there are the costs of consultants for businesses to figure out their own healthcare expenses and options for their benefit programs, brokers, state government personnel to keep track of each insurance company, and hospital and other institutional personnel to negotiate and keep up with individual insurer contracts. The $400 billion of excess expenses and profits could certainly be used more effectively. This level of savings is attainable, but it will take great courage and effort.

A Brief Discussion Regarding Life Expectancy

Hundreds, if not thousands, of articles have been written about the fact that the life expectancy in the U.S. is lower than in many other industrialized countries despite higher healthcare costs. For example, Japan spent about $2,249 per person and had an average life expectancy of 82 years in 2004. By comparison, the U.S. spent about $6,100 per person with a life expectancy of 78 years. Much has been made of this discrepancy, and authors have pointed to this as further "proof" that we, in the U.S., are not "getting our money's worth". On the surface, that argument sounds correct. Like everything else, however, there is another side to the issue.[10]

The U.S. population consists of about 300 million people, of which about 115 million are either uninsured, underinsured, or on Medicaid. As previously demonstrated, the uninsured are at significantly higher risk of dying in the hospital, having more advanced diseases, not receiving adequate preventive care, not having the finances to purchase appropriate medications, etc. Much of the same is true for the Medicaid population and to a lesser extent the underinsured. Intuitively, one would expect that these three groups should have a lower life expectancy than the rest of the population.

In fact, two studies looking at this problem over a total of twenty years found that patients without health insurance had a 25–50% greater chance of dying than their counterparts who had *private* insurance. These results took into consideration any statistical difference in the disease status of the individuals at the outset of the study period, thereby leaving the presence or absence of private insurance as the only variable. Patients with public insurance (Medicare, Medicaid, disability insurance, Indian Health

Service, etc.) were all excluded. The study by McWilliams stated that the lack of insurance was responsible for about 13,000 excess deaths annually in the age group 55 to 64 and estimated that number to be about 30,000 per year by 2015. Lack of insurance was the third leading cause of death behind heart disease and cancer![11, 12] Although there is no data on the life expectancy of Medicaid patients or the underinsured, I believe it is quite likely that they also have a poor overall prognosis as a result of inferior preventive care and all the issues described above.

If we compare the lower life expectancy in the U.S. to Japan (which has the highest life expectancy in the world) on a simple mathematical basis, we can easily understand the reason for the difference. Assuming that the two-thirds of the population that has health insurance (private and Medicare) has the same life expectancy as Japan, what would the life expectancy of the other one-third have to be to pull us down to where we actually are?

$$\text{U.S. life expectancy} = .66 \times (\text{Japan}) + .33 \times (\text{uninsured})$$
$$78 = .66 \times 82 + .33 \times 72$$

This means that the one-third of the U.S. population that is uninsured, on Medicaid, or underinsured would have an average life expectancy of about 72 years. Is this plausible? Can the absence of good healthcare shorten your life by ten years? This would be comparable to life expectancies in many eastern European and South American countries. I believe this is conceivable.

It is also possible that an average 82 years survival in the U.S. is not realistic for this example (for 2004 data) even with adequate insurance coverage, in view of our genetic makeup and lifestyle, which are different from those in Japan. If we insert 80 or 81 years instead of 82 (which may be more realistic), that makes the estimated life expectancy of the one-third without insurance 75 or 76, which is perhaps more believable. Additional factors such as the frequency of "illnesses of choice", HIV/AIDS, crime rates, accidental deaths, attitudes toward healthcare, and genetic differences also play a significant role in establishing the average life span for a country.

In any event, a major determinant of life expectancy is whether the individual has *private* health insurance, which will provide access to preventive medicine, timely care of illnesses, and proper drug therapy as needed.

One could, therefore, make the argument that the reduced life expectancy of our society is significantly impacted by the lack of universal health coverage and, therefore, people are needlessly dying prematurely. In a country that spends such a huge amount on healthcare, it is difficult to understand why we cannot reapportion the money to provide comprehensive medical care for all.

The Short Story

Of the categories discussed above, the only two that can realistically create any meaningful savings are: 1) changes in financing of the uninsured, underinsured, and Medicaid, and 2) healthcare administrative costs. These two categories together could save about $460 billion per year in 2004 dollars. Additionally, the cost of drugs can be brought down by allowing importation from other countries that have favorable pricing compared to the U.S. Obviously, safeguards would be needed to protect the public from counterfeit or tainted pharmaceuticals. Other countries have achieved these safeguards. If some element of parallel trade were to be allowed or encouraged in the U.S., costs would decrease appreciably. Additionally, allowing larger negotiating groups would improve pricing. If this were to occur, the savings would be about 30% or $60 billion.

The Big Picture

So where are we in practical terms?

- Our existing financing system leaves more than one-third of the population either uninsured, underinsured, or covered by a Medicaid system that all believe is ineffective, inefficient, very costly, and providing poor healthcare. Any one of us, or someone in our extended family, could be included in these very unfortunate categories of poor healthcare delivery through no fault of our own. Even if we are not directly affected by one or more of these groups, overhauling the system will save all of us a great sum of money. If not for altruism, then certainly for selfish reasons, we should strive to correct the existing healthcare financing and delivery system for these groups of people.

- The uninsured, underinsured, and the Medicaid population need to be provided with standard, comprehensive private health insurance supporting reasonable provider (physician and hospital) reimbursements. The cost of this can be significantly lower than the current expenses if the overhead of the insurance coverage is kept low, as in the Medicare program, and if appropriate care is delivered in the correct setting.

- There will be increasing numbers of people who are uninsured and underinsured as the cost of healthcare increases. We will all continue to pay for this through federal and state programs with ever-increasing taxes and higher private insurance premiums.

- We could save some money by opening up more price competition in the drug industry. It would be reasonable to expect a 30% reduction in drug cost for a $60 billion annual savings.

- We cannot wring out enough money from the physician and hospital fee structures to make a great difference in overall spending without harming the system. The vast majority of those payments go toward salaries, and there is an existing, as well as a future, serious shortage of skilled personnel. Reducing salaries will only make this worse by decreasing the number and/or quality of workers.

- Medical malpractice tort reform, though necessary in my opinion, will not produce significant savings in the near future.

- More attention to disease management programs, though beneficial and very important, will likely not reduce costs and may actually increase expenditures.

- The huge administrative costs of private insurers can only be reduced effectively by switching to a single-payer system. One would think that with at least 115 million people on Medicaid, uninsured, and underinsured, as well as forty-three million enrolled in the Medicare program already—amounting to more than one-half of our population—there would be enough support for a single-payer system in the form of "Universal" Medicare to make this a reality. The people at risk (uninsured, underinsured, and Medicaid) probably do not have enough political clout to effect change. They are not organized, they do not contribute to political campaigns, and they are generally marginalized in our society. They need an organization like the Gray Panthers of many years ago to shape their message and make a political impact.

There is no impetus for the Medicare population to get involved with this cause since they already have adequate health coverage except for drugs. A coalition of these groups would be very effective. In the absence of this scenario, achieving change will require a groundswell of support from 50% of the population actually paying for healthcare through taxes and private insurance premiums. This will occur when the financial pain of the existing system is unbearable, a situation we appear to be nearing.

- The solutions to the financing problem are available to us wherein we can save in excess of $522 billion per year by overhauling the administrative costs, providing coverage that is not only less expensive but also superior for the indigent, as well as lowering drug pricing.

- The expenses of "illnesses of choice" (about $220 billion) need to be addressed so that these patients take more personal responsibility for their actions and are therefore incentivized to improve their health status.

- Physicians and other providers need to be mindful of their obligations to practice high-quality, cost-effective medicine while being sure that the patient's health is not compromised.

- Insurance companies and the federal government have focused on ways to reduce the reimbursements to physicians and hospitals, provide less coverage, and increase deductibles and copayments that do not get to the root cause of the problem. These "cost-saving" measures are also leading to an increase in the number of uninsured, higher premiums for less coverage, and higher out-of-pocket payments for people with insurance. These ill-conceived strategies only foment anger, discontent, and despair among those who are trying to provide a caring and professional atmosphere for our patients and do nothing to promote improved healthcare.

- We need a more meaningful debate in this country based upon actual facts regarding how our money is being spent, who is benefiting from the expenditures, where the waste is, how and where costs can be controlled, and whether we have the will to make the hard choices and decisions necessary to bring the costs down and provide better care for everyone. Do we want to spend large sums of money on needless administrative expenses and high private insurance overhead or on quality care for all? Our system will likely never be as inexpensive as the rest of the world in view of our salary structure, but we can certainly reduce the expenditures substantially as indicated in the preceding chapters. It is time to stop "trimming around the edges" and take up the key issues relating to the expenses of our healthcare system. If we are not willing to do this, we should put the discussion to rest and silently endure the ever-increasing price of healthcare.

- It is time to press our national leaders for explanations and bold decisions to improve our system. This book has been designed to provide the knowledge base that will enable us to ask the right questions and have the necessary debate in our country to accomplish these goals. Our healthcare system is truly on life support, and if we do not take bold steps in the very near future, the patient will die!

EPILOGUE

———————————————

I have tried to set forth the financial issues confronting the U.S. healthcare system in an objective format so that everyone can understand and be able to engage in a meaningful dialogue regarding how to fix the system or, at the very least, express their views and desires rationally. As this discussion draws to a close, I believe there is a need for me to explain where I stand on these issues as a practicing physician, a consumer of health services, and a citizen who pays taxes.

When I started to think about the issues of healthcare financing in a global fashion several years ago, I was struck, as many of us have been, by the enormous disparity between the U.S. and the rest of the world. As a former engineer, I believe there is a logical, mathematical explanation for everything. I thought if I could just peel back the layers of this complex problem in a non-biased fashion, I could find the "truth" and explain the differences. I took the position, having read medical literature for more than thirty-five years, that we as a society—the medical "industry" itself, most specifically—have not been providing healthcare dramatically differently by comparison to any other industrialized country. Physicians have all taken care of patients in a relatively similar manner from a medical standpoint. There were no miracle cures that physicians in other countries have had that we did not. Information has been shared openly and generally without bias among the countries of the world. We have all learned from one another's experiences. So why should we be spending more than twice on healthcare than other industrialized countries? I felt that analyzing all the components of the system would have to yield a logical explanation, which would then enable us to find the "answer" and ultimately to fix the problem. Most books and articles have dealt with one or two highly-charged issues (pharmaceutical and insurance company profiteering, poor healthcare for the indigent, the growing uninsured population) that have been sensationalized, but a comprehensive analysis has not been set forth.

As a physician, I believe it is my duty to heal and care for people regardless of their financial status and ability to pay. I do this every day in my practice. Having said that, there is still a need for physicians to earn enough money to pay for our offices, staff, malpractice and health insurance, supplies, etc. Likewise, hospitals have the same obligations and responsibilities.

I also believe that comprehensive healthcare is a "right", and the U.S. is surprisingly alone in the industrialized world in not accepting this premise. This country takes the position that healthcare is a commodity that you can purchase if you have enough money.

In 1948, the United Nations General Assembly adopted the Universal Declaration of Human Rights, which states in Article 25:

(1) Everyone has the right to a standard of living adequate for the health and well-being of himself and of his family, including food, clothing, housing and medical care and necessary social services, and the right to security in the event of unemployment, sickness, disability, widowhood, old age or other lack of livelihood in circumstances beyond his control.

(2) Motherhood and childhood are entitled to special care and assistance. All children, whether born in or out of wedlock, shall enjoy the same social protection.

Furthermore, in an effort to explain and enhance the Universal Declaration of Human Rights, the U.N. General Assembly, in 1966, also adopted the International Covenant on Economic, Social and Cultural Rights, which states, in Article 12:

(1) The States Parties to the present Covenant recognize the right of everyone to the enjoyment of the highest attainable standard of physical and mental health.

(2) The steps to be taken by the States Parties to the present Covenant to achieve the full realization of this right shall include those necessary for:

    (a) The provision for the reduction of the stillbirth-rate and of infant mortality and for the healthy development of the child;

    (b) The improvement of all aspects of environmental and industrial hygiene;

    (c) The prevention, treatment and control of epidemic, endemic, occupational and other diseases;

    (d) The creation of conditions which would assure to all medical service and medical attention in the event of sickness.

Although it is true that some of the general precepts of these declarations are in effect in the U.S. (we have some prenatal and perinatal programs for the indigent, industrial health and OSHA, and public health programs for disease prevention and treatment of epidemics), we do not provide for (1) or (2d), and (2a) is poorly done for the indigent. Actually, the U.S. is one of six countries of the 155 in the U.N. that has not yet ratified the covenant, so one could argue that we are not bound by its provisions. We are, however, in the company of South Africa, Sao Tome, Pakistan, Laos, and Belize.

We do not provide healthcare to the Medicaid population, the uninsured, and the underinsured according to the U.N. resolutions. The people receive their care in the most inefficient fashion possible, in the emergency rooms of our hospitals, costing many times what it would to be seen in a physician's office. They lack any reasonable preventive and follow-up care, and the care itself is often demeaning. They often cannot afford to purchase needed medication and will go without necessary services that could be lifesaving because of their inability to pay for them. As a result, they have a higher mortality rate than the rest of the population (10–15% greater) and an even higher incidence of cardiovascular mortality (up to 50% higher).[1] Furthermore, as indicated earlier, these poor health conditions cause increased absenteeism from work and tens of billions of dollars of lost productivity annually since more than two-thirds of the uninsured are employed. They also have a 10–28% reduction in earnings as a result of poor health, further increasing the downward spiral of their inability to pay for healthcare. These people are not politically organized and therefore are unable to mount a lobbying effort that will make a significant impact on legislators. Be aware that if the Medicare population were to align itself with the poor, that would represent in excess of 50% of our population and would be a major force with which to contend.

Many—perhaps most—of us who are insured don't really care about the plight of the uninsured, underinsured, or the Medicaid population because they are "out of sight and out of mind". We might get a little worked up periodically when a new report comes out about the growing number of uninsured in the country (as long as we are not part of it) or when federal and state taxes go up to pay for Medicaid or the uninsured. But, in general, we don't think about it too much. After all, the uninsured and the Medicaid patients get all the care they need in our country's emergency rooms, hospitals, and doctors' offices, don't they? Somehow this gets paid for, and all is well with the world.

Well, maybe not.

I have always tried to abide by a philosophy when dealing with other people to be fair and look at their side of the situation. It is usually reasonable to have one person cut the pie and have the other person pick which piece he or she wants. In that way, you can be sure that each side has equal opportunity. This does not seem to be the case when dealing with healthcare financing. We need to design a system in which all people get a fair shake.

One very compelling reason for us to fashion a more compassionate and humane system is that any one of us can become uninsured or underinsured at any time. I have friends, acquaintances, and patients who were flying high in various businesses and occupations and, for any one of several reasons, suddenly found themselves out of work. It is often very difficult to find an adequate replacement job. Downsizing of a company or industry reduces the number of job offerings. Having healthcare insurance when you are out of work usually entails purchasing COBRA. The next job, if available, could be one based upon commissions without health insurance, with a small company that does not offer health insurance, or with one that requires a long waiting period before being insured. COBRA is not cheap; but when it runs out in eighteen months, you could be looking to purchase private family health insurance, which is *extremely* expensive. Not a pretty sight. If you decide not to purchase insurance, a major illness, like a heart attack, or an auto accident could cause overwhelming bills and bankruptcy. This is a real threat facing millions of Americans each day. Two recent studies estimated the frequency of bankruptcy from a medical illness was 17–55%. The large spread is a result of one study being from a more liberal vantage point and the other a more conservative viewpoint.[2, 3] In both cases, however, the numbers were not insignificant. I recognize that true "captains of industry" will likely never face this potential problem; but the rest of us, with good jobs, could certainly have the rug pulled out from under us at any time.

Even if you don't go bankrupt, the ever-increasing expenditures for deductibles, copayments, employee contributions to health insurance premiums, and the cost of prescription medications will undoubtedly eat into your disposable income. Furthermore, as your personal contribution to healthcare expenses increases, the amount of financial liability that the insurer and your employer face decreases. How long do you think this process of shifting the risk to you will have to go on before you are unable to afford reasonable healthcare and still have money left over for you and your family? This discussion regarding the potentially devastating financial consequences of our existing system really only pertains to the "other guy" and not you, right? So who cares? There are very few patients, if any, in my practice and very few of my friends who think the current situation and the future prospects are reasonable or acceptable.

If altruism toward others and your risk of financial ruin are not reason enough to want dramatic change in the healthcare financing system, let's look at *additional* self-interest. It *is* possible that the scenario described above could be your future. Let's assume, however, that is not likely and look at the costs you are shouldering by paying for private health insurance:

- First, your premiums are rising about 35% faster than the actual cost of healthcare.
- Second, you are paying an additional $341 for individual and $922 for family health insurance per year to offset what the uninsured are not paying.

- Third, your health insurance is also paying an additional $27 billion annually to cover hospital underpayments by Medicare and Medicaid.
- Fourth, you are paying your share of the taxes to cover the $300 billion per year—and growing—cost for Medicaid (half at the federal level and half at the state level).
- Fifth, you are paying state taxes to support "charity" care to hospitals, which in New Jersey alone was about $500 million in 2005.
- Sixth, you are paying state, county, and local taxes for the support of indigent care clinics.
- Seventh, you are paying your share of about $420 billion per year for the administration of the entire healthcare system or about $1,400 per year per person more than Canada. Included in this number are the bloated costs of the private insurance companies together with their profits, huge management salaries and stock options, the corporate jet, and the vast army of people working for the companies in excess of the number required by a single-payer system. Furthermore, there are the commissions for insurance agents, consultants, the hundreds of diverse computer systems, and so on and so on.

If private insurers had the overhead of Medicare, the savings would be, in aggregate, about $120 billion per year.

If Medicaid were funded properly, these patients would obtain care in a doctor's office (not the ER), and the savings could be about $50 billion per year.

Furthermore, the overcrowding of the nation's emergency rooms would radically decrease so that when *you* have *your* heart attack, the closest ER will not be on "divert", or closed to any new admissions, and you will receive prompt life-saving care.

If we total the "waste", we come up with potential savings of about $2,000 per person per year.[4] This number will only increase annually as more people become uninsured or go on to Medicaid as a result of increasing private healthcare premiums and more employers eliminating this benefit. Additionally, it is unlikely that administrative costs will decrease with so many people feeding at the trough, requiring cost-of-living salary increases, all of which will be passed on to the consumer: you.

The problem of waste as a result of the uninsured, underinsured, and Medicaid seems obvious. We are paying taxes and extra private health insurance premiums to support a system of care for the indigent that could be handled far better and for much less money if all of "them" had standard comprehensive healthcare coverage and received appropriate care in the appropriate setting.

The next huge issue is the cost of administering the existing healthcare system. Just follow the money. You and/or your employer pay private insurance premiums (which, by the way, leave large out-of-pocket costs for you). The companies take this money and pay out 80% of it for your healthcare. Part of the 80% that is paid to providers like hospitals, nursing homes, home care, and physicians on your behalf goes to the high administrative overhead of each of these groups, in large part created by the need to deal with hundreds of insurers and the hugely redundant bureaucracy. The remaining 20% is retained by the insurance company. You do remember the 22.6 employees/10,000 enrollees figure from before, the duplication of the billing systems, the executive salaries, the corporate jet, and the profits that go to the shareholders? It just seems to me that if the healthcare premium dollar is so costly and sacred, as we have all declared, we should not permit these large amounts to be spent on anything but the provision of healthcare. All efforts should be undertaken to rid the system of any payments and expenses superfluous to those necessary to keep us healthy. Insurance company waste and profit should not be part of the equation.

The wasteful, bloated, redundant healthcare system we had prior to the dominance of our existing managed care system has been replaced by the wasteful, bloated, redundant, and hugely profitable private insurance managed care system. We have exchanged one problem for another without much net gain and have created a great deal of dissatisfaction among patients and providers of care alike.

Additionally, is it okay for us to pay almost twice the per unit dose cost for drugs compared to the other industrialized countries? Should we continue to pay for the R and D of the entire world? There is no justification for this. The cost of drugs can come down dramatically if we adopt competitive principles similar to those of other countries.

Would you rather continue to pay in excess of $2,000 more per year per person for the inefficiencies of our system, or do you think there needs to be a radical change? I can't imagine anyone is happy with the status quo, except the insurers and the pharmaceutical companies. Whether you are guided by altruism or self-interest, the net result is the same. The system is broken, and it desperately needs to be fixed.

When I began research for this manuscript, I had no preconceived notion as to why U.S. expenses were so high compared to those of the rest of the world or what the solution might be. I just wanted to try to apply simple math to the problem and to figure the whole thing out. As I uncovered information and continued to "peel back the onion", it became more and more obvious what the causes were and what the solutions would have to be. I don't see any way around creating a single-payer system and using it as the nucleus of a new healthcare program for all (universal healthcare), in addition to the other ideas and remedies outlined in the previous chapters.

There are several terms that have, unfortunately, been used interchangeably to describe this type of healthcare system. They include "single-payer", "universal", "single-risk pool", and "socialized medicine". They all mean something different, but they can all be used together to define a type of healthcare delivery. "Single-payer" means that one entity (government or private) collects the money from premiums or taxation and also pays the fees to the providers. This allows for maximum efficiency without redundancy on the administrative side. "Universal" means that *all* people within our country will be covered by the same insurance program. "Single-risk pool" means that all the people within the coverage program (all people in our country) will share the financial upside and downside of insuring everyone. Actuarially, the larger the number of people within the pool, the safer we are since the downside or "risk" is spread over a very large number of people. So, therefore, I believe that the best approach for us is to create a *universal healthcare, single-payer, single-risk pool system.*

The major opposition to this type of delivery system is the notion that it is "socialized medicine". In reality, it would be no more "socialized medicine" than the existing Medicare program. The term "socialized medicine" gets thrown around a lot in this type of discussion. Various definitions have been offered:

- Any of various systems designed to provide the entire population with complete medical care through government subsidization and regularization of medical and health services.[5]
- A government-regulated system for providing healthcare for all by means of subsidies derived from taxation.[6]

- A system for providing medical and hospital care for all at a nominal cost by means of government regulation of health services and subsidies derived from taxation.[7]
- Medical and hospital services for the members of a class or population administered by an organized group (such as a state agency) and paid for from funds obtained usually by assessments, philanthropy, or taxation.[8]

Wikipedia offers a different take on the definition:

Socialized medicine is a somewhat pejorative phrase first popularized in 1920s and 1930s United States politics by conservative opponents of publicly operated health care, proposed during the administration of U. S. President Franklin Roosevelt and later championed by U. S. Sen. Spessard Holland of Florida, Sen. Estes Kefauver of Tennessee and many more. Organizations that generally oppose expansion of government services still tend to use the phrase in that way. However, others have pointed out that the United States government already operates public health care. That approach to health care is provided by U. S. Veterans Administration clinics and hospitals to former members of U. S. military services.

The common threads are that there is healthcare for all and that it is run by and *regulated* by the government. The major complaint from people who oppose this type of system is that it is *regulated* by the government. They fear that government intrusion will cause loss of choices on several levels: by patients regarding doctors and hospitals and by physicians regarding types of therapy and testing as well as drugs prescribed. There is also a fear of losing existing doctor-patient relationships. Furthermore, the fear of underfunding the entire system that could lead to long waiting lists for care is a significant concern. Well, frankly, I have not heard that type of criticism of the Medicare program (except from patients in the *managed* Medicare programs run by the private insurance companies); but I have heard, and continue to hear, that precise criticism of the existing managed care delivery system that we have today! Every day multiple private insurance patients complain to me about their health insurance. They are annoyed that they require referrals to see specialists, annoyed about restrictions regarding which hospital or physician they can see depending upon if they are "in network", annoyed about restrictions regarding the use of certain medications that may not be "on formulary" with their insurer, and annoyed that their physician is often not permitted to order a test that the physician believes is necessary. I never hear this from Medicare patients. Every system will have some regulation, but experience tells us that Medicare is *far less* regulated than our current managed care system that we seem to be protecting! I do not understand this. The managed care industry has used very slanted commercials (some would call it propaganda) in print, radio, and television media to convince us that a single-payer, universal, single-risk pool system is dangerous and will limit choice, etc. This is all self-interest on the part of insurance companies. They stand to lose a great deal of money and are fighting for their lives. What they are saying, however, is not true. Just ask your relatives who are on Medicare.

I agree with critics of a single-payer system who do not want the government in total control of healthcare so that we do not, for instance, fall victim to the negative aspects of the Canadian and the United Kingdom systems. We obviously do not want loss of competition among hospitals and physicians over quality and accessibility. We don't want long waiting lines for care. We have all heard of the patients in Canada who have had to wait for months to have an MRI or coronary bypass surgery, some of whom have died waiting. These problems have occurred as a result of provincial and national budgets so that hospitals and physicians have no incentive to provide timely care. Once again, I am not advocating that type of system. Rather, I am in favor of a single-payer system that collects money from taxation and pays for the healthcare services rendered that are at the *sole* discretion of the physician and the patient for whom he is providing the care. The *provision* of care should be on a "free enterprise" basis with competition among providers; but the waste, redundancy, corporate profiteering, and inefficiency should be removed. Nothing more and nothing less. Medicare for all. It will save money, provide care for all, and be a more humane way to deliver healthcare.

What is the practical answer to this problem of bringing costs down to where they should be and improving the delivery system? In my opinion, there are several principles that must be incorporated into any system that is designed to improve care and costs:

- There must be comprehensive health coverage for *all*: "universal coverage".

- There must be a single-risk pool, meaning the entire population is in one program. This will eliminate the huge administrative costs of the private insurers and avoid the ability of the private insurers to "cherry-pick" the healthiest in our population and leave the sicker patients for the government program. You need the whole population in a single pool to spread out the risk among *all* three hundred million people to keep the costs per person low. This "cherry-picking" scheme was executed successfully by some of the HMOs several years ago.

- To ensure fairness and adequacy of coverage, the entire population, including *all* legislators, governors, and other elected officials, will be in the system. It should also be illegal to pay separately for any care within the package or to obtain preferential care.

- Coverage should be comprehensive so that all medically necessary care is provided, as in the existing Medicare program.

- Covered services will be delineated by expert panels in each specialty, without governmental interference, similar to the Medicare program. Covered services will be standardized across the country without the existing regional differences.

- Deductibles and copayments should be eliminated. This is controversial, and some provision may be needed for income-adjusted payments.

- Prescription drugs should be covered with no extra cost. Again, there may need to be income-adjusted payments.

- Private insurance companies will not be allowed to sell health insurance for this comprehensive coverage package but will be permitted to sell coverage for extras such as plastic surgery and other discretionary procedures. This will allow them to remain viable and give them a niche within which to function.

- The system will be administered similar to Medicare with freedom of choice of physician and hospital.

- Care will be paid for on a fee-for-service basis. Fees will be fair and reasonable and will be increased annually based upon inflation costs. Hospitals will no longer be shortchanged.

- The system will negotiate pricing with drug and device companies on behalf of all of us to gain market power. This will level the playing field with the rest of the world and cause the companies to decrease our costs while, perhaps, increasing prices elsewhere to maintain the necessary margins for R and D and profit.

- Financing this system will be through taxation based upon income for individuals and employers. Individuals could pay a tax similar to Medicare, based upon income, and/or corporations could also be taxed based upon gross salary expenditures. The precise formulas will require actuarial input. Since *all* workers and employers will contribute, as opposed to the current system in which many employers and individuals do not contribute, there will be a more equitable distribution of contributory payments. In many instances, the costs per person will decrease.

- Billing from and payments to providers will be made through one national computer system network, which will reduce the complexity and costs of the current redundant systems.

- There will be a standardized computer network nationwide for physicians and hospitals that will be a repository of all patient information with software that will improve quality and reduce errors. Obviously, personal information safeguards will be necessary to avoid unauthorized access. The federal government will pay for the establishment and maintenance of the system.

- Tort reform will be enacted in the form of a compromise that will protect patients' rights but reduce or eliminate the current "lottery" system of jury verdicts.

- Patients with "illnesses of choice" will be charged a higher premium for care.

- Provider entrepreneurial spirit will be encouraged so that creativity will be enhanced.

This proposed "universal coverage, single-payer, single-risk pool" system is achievable and represents the fairest and most cost-effective financing and delivery system for all Americans. This is not "socialism". There should be no global or regional budgeting as is currently the case in several other countries such as Canada and the U.K. As a result, we can have a healthcare financing system similar to the Medicare system that we now enjoy, in which providers are encouraged to compete on access and quality. The entrepreneurial spirit is strong, and innovations have taken place for forty years.

The type of fundamental change articulated above will be opposed by the insurance and pharmaceutical companies, as well as by all those who participate in consulting, advertising, and other types of work for the existing healthcare delivery system. To implement this new structure of healthcare, great courage and determination will be needed by legislators, and we, the public, need to bring enough knowledge and pressure to bear on the discussions to make change possible. We just need to do the math and allow altruism and/or self-interest to govern our decisions.

The time has come to learn about the healthcare system and then decide how to finance it. If we abrogate our responsibility to learn, discuss, and make a difference, we will have no one to blame but ourselves. Our existing system is on "life support", and the patient is terminal. Any one of us can be my patient whom we met in the introduction to this book. Any one of us can be "Roger"!

WHAT YOU CAN DO

Once you have a clear understanding of the healthcare system, I encourage you to discuss the problems with everyone you know! Start a grassroots dialogue and engage your federal legislators in the discussions. Send email questions and opinions to those inside the Washington, D.C. beltway and to your state legislators and governors so they understand your personal concerns and desires. Tell them stories of your experiences and those of your friends and relatives. Government officials, both state and federal, will be very interested in your concerns. Additionally, many state governments are now seeking ways to resolve the healthcare financing crisis (notably California, Massachusetts, Pennsylvania, and Maine). Others will likely follow the lead of these states. This gives you an excellent opportunity to have a more local impact on the problem. You can pointedly ask your state and federal legislators why we are the only country in the industrialized world that has a system that does not provide *comprehensive* healthcare for *all*. Tell them we need serious, radical changes and not merely trimming around the edges. Explain to them that there is a way to pay for this entire program of "universal healthcare" and still save money. It is possible!

SOURCES OF INFORMATION

In an effort to develop an even greater understanding of the issues involving healthcare financing and delivery, the following list of websites is being provided for you to access for additional information. They are excellent resources and provide information on all aspects of the discussion.

An organization known as the "Center for Healthcare Finance Information" has been formed. Its mission is to concisely bring important facts to public awareness, which will be updated frequently. The Center collects newly published information from many sources and forms links to this information for easy access. You can reach this important website at: www.health-financing.com.

Alliance for Health Reform: www.allhealth.org

American Student Medical Association: www.amsa.org/uhc/uhcres.cfm

Center for Studying Health System Change: www.hschange.org

Centers for Medicare and Medicaid Services: www.cms.gov

The Commonwealth Fund: www.cmwf.org

Everybody in, nobody out: www.everybodyinnobodyout.org

Families USA: www.familiesusa.org

Health Affairs: www.healthaffairs.org

The Heritage Foundation: www.heritage.org

Institute of Medicine: www.iom.edu

Kaiser Family Foundation: www.kff.org

New England Journal of Medicine: www.nejm.org

Organization for Economic Cooperation and Development: www.oecd.org

Physicians for a National Health Program: www.pnhp.org

President Bush's Healthcare Agenda: www.whitehouse.gov/stateoftheunion/2006/healthcare/index.html

Public Citizen: www.citizen.org

The Right to Health Care…now!: www.righttohealthcare.org

Web MD: www.webmd.com

World Health Organization: www.who.int/en

Contacts

U.S. House of Representatives: www.house.gov

U.S. Senate: www.senate.gov

The White House: www.whitehouse.gov

NOTES

Chapter 1

1. "OECD Health Data 2005," Organization for Economic Cooperation and Development http://oecd.org/.

2. Anderson, Gerard F. "It's the Prices, Stupid: Why the United States Is So Different from Other Countries," *Health Affairs* 22 (2003): 89–105.

3. Ibid.

4. Canadian Institute for Health Information, http://www.cihi.ca.

5. U.S. expenditures for 2003 = $1.7T. Administration costs are 31% = $539 billion or $1,822/person. Canada expenditures for 2003 = $122 billion. Administration costs are 16.7% = $20.5 billion or $650/person. This is $524 PPP U.S. Difference is $1298/person. Canadian enhanced expense is $1298 x 31.6 million =$41 billion.

6. Barham, Leela. "Comparing Physicians' Earnings: Current Knowledge and Challenges: A Final Report for the Department of Health," NERA Economic Consulting, 2004.

7. "Health Care in Canada 2004," Canadian Institute for Health Information, http://www.cihi.ca.

8. Bodenheimer, Thomas, MD. "High and Rising Health Care Costs. Part 3: The Role of Health Care Providers," *Annals of Internal Medicine* 142 (2005): 996–1002.

9. Danzon, Patricia. "Prices and Availability of Pharmaceuticals: Evidence from Nine Countries," *Health Affairs*. (2003): Web Exclusive W3 521–536.

10. Ibid.

11. Canadian Institute for Health Information, http://www.cihi.ca.

12. "Health Care in Canada 2005," Canadian Institute for Health Information, http://www.cihi.ca.

13. Canadian Statistics—Earnings, average weekly, by industry, http://www.statcan.ca (accessed May 19, 2006).

14. "National Compensation Survey: Occupational Wages in the United States, July, 2004," U.S. Department of Labor, August 2005.

15. Average non-nurse professional salaries = $23.91. Average nurse salary = $26.60. Average hourly salary = $25.25.

16. See #4.

Chapter 2

1. Reinhardt, Uwe. "Cross-National Comparisons of Health Systems Using OECD Data, 1999," *Health Affairs* (2002): 169–181.

2. Ibid.

3. "Where's the stick?" *Economist,* October 11, 2003.

4. "List of countries by income equality," Wikipedia, http://wikipedia.org/.

5. Reinhardt, "Cross-National Comparisons."

6. "National Compensation Survey: Occupational Wages in the United States, July, 2004," U.S. Department of Labor, August 2005.

7. Jolly, Paul. "Medical School Tuition And Young Physicians' Indebtedness," *Health Affairs* 24 (2005): 527–535.

8. Weeks, William. "A Comparison of the Educational Costs and Incomes of Physicians and Other Professionals," *The New England Journal of Medicine* 330 (1994): 1280–1286.

9. "Multimillion-dollar makeover." *American Medical News,* December 12, 2005, Professional Issues Section.

10. Barham, Leela. "Comparing Physicians' Earnings: Current Knowledge and Challenges: A Final Report for the Department of Health," NERA Economic Consulting, 2004.

11. Canadian Statistics—Earnings, average weekly, by industry, http://www.statcan.ca (accessed May 19, 2006).

12. "National Compensation Survey: Occupational Wages in the United States, July, 2004," U.S. Department of Labor, August 2005.

13. 2004 Survey of Physicians Fifty to Sixty-Five Years Old, Merritt, Hawkins and Associates, 2005.

14. Association of American Medical Colleges, http://www.aamc.org/.

15. Cooper, Richard. "Scarce Physicians Encounter Scarce Foundations: A Call for Action," *Health Affairs* 23 (2004): 243–249.

16. Frye, W. Bruce. "Cardiology Workforce: A Shortage, Not a Surplus," *Health Affairs* (2004): Web Exclusive W4 64–66.

17. Spetz, Joanne. "The Future of the Nurse Shortage: Will Wage Increase Close the Gap?" *Health Affairs* 22 (2003): 199–206.

18. Spetz, Joanne. "How Can Employment-Based Benefits Help the Nurse Shortage?" *Health Affairs* 25 (2006): 212–218.

19. Hassmiller, Susan. "Addressing the Nurse Shortage to Improve the Quality of Patient Care," *Health Affairs* 25 (2006): 268–274.

20.

2004			
	Dollars in Billions	% salaries	Salaries in Dollars in Billions
Hospital	571	70.00%	399.7
Professional	587	72.00%	422.64
Nursing Homes	158	70.00%	110.6
Drugs/supplies	243		
Administration	137		
Investment	125		
Public Health	56	70.00%	39.2
Total	1877		972.14
% salaries			51.79%

21. Weiss, Gail, "Expense Survey: What It Costs To Practice Today," *Medical Economics,* December 9, 2002.

22. Tu, Ha. "Losing Ground: Physician Income, 1995–2003, Tracking Study No. 15," Center for Studying Health System Change, http://www.hschange.org/.

23. Ibid.

24. Data Bulletin No. 24, March 2003. "Behind the Times: Physician Income, 1995–99," Center for Studying Health System Change, http://www.hschange.org (accessed December 23, 2003).

25. *Medical Economics.* http://www.memag.com/.

26. Tu, Ha.

27. Hadley, Jack. "How Much Medical Care Do the Uninsured Use, and Who Pays for It?" *Health Affairs* (2003): Web Exclusive W3 66–81.

28. Zuckerman, Stephen. "Changes In Medicaid Physician Fees, 1998–2003: Implications For Physician Participation," *Health Affairs* (2004): Web Exclusive W4 374–84.

29. Landers, Susan. "Monitoring dose crucial for anticoagulants," *American Medical News*, July 3, 2006, Health and Science Section.

Chapter 3

1. "Quarterly Index Levels in the CMS (IPPS) Hospital 2002," Centers for Medicare and Medicaid Services, http://www.cms.gov/.

2. Joint Committee on Public Health, Massachusetts Association of Health Plans, October 19, 2005.

3. "Nursing Shortage Fact Sheet," June 14, 2006, American Association of Colleges of Nursing, http://www.aacn.nche.edu/.

4. "Nursing Facts: Nursing Shortage," February 2006, American Nurses Association, http://www.nursingworld.org/.

5. "The State of American Hospitals—Taking the Pulse 2006," American Hospital Association, http://www.aha.org/.

6. "National Uncompensated Care Based on Cost: 1980–2004," November 2005, American Hospital Association, http://www.aha.org/.

7. "Hospital ad spending," *American Medical News,* February 27, 2006, Quickview.

8. Table 97. "Health, United States, 2005," Centers for Medicare and Medicaid Services, http://www.cms.gov/.

9. "Total Inpatient Days in Community Hospitals 1981–2004, Trendwatch Chartbook 2006," American Hospital Association, http://www.aha.org/.

10. "Inpatient hospitalizations in Canada increase slightly after many years of decline," November 30, 2005, Canadian Institute for Health Information, http://www.cihi.ca/.

Chapter 4

1. "Competition in Health Insurance: A Comprehensive Study of U.S. Markets 2005 Update," American Medical Association, http://www.ama-assn.org/.

2. "Announced Hospital Mergers and Acquisitions 1998–2004, Trendwatch Chartbook 2006," American Hospital Association, http://www.aha.org/.

3. Bodenheimer MD, Thomas. "High and Rising Health Care Costs. Part 1: Seeking an Explanation," *Annals of Internal Medicine* 142 (2005): 847–854.

4. Green, Meg. "Big, better, best? Even as some insurers gain national size through mergers and acquisitions, competition is still a local battle," The Foundation for Taxpayer and Consumer Rights, http://www.consumerwatchdog.org/.

5. Bethely, Jonathan. "Health plans make more, spend less in 2005," *American Medical News,* March 6, 2006, 30.

6. "Top Dollar: CEO Compensation in Medicare's Private Insurance Plans, June, 2003," Families USA, http://www.familiesusa.org/.

7. "HMO Plan Median Operating Margins 1990–2004, Trendwatch Chartbook 2006," American Hospital Association, http://www.aha.org/.

8. "Operating Margins of the Top Insurers 2000–2004, Trendwatch Chartbook 2006," American Hospital Association, http://www.aha.org/.

9. Woolhandler, Steffie. "Costs of Health Care Administration in the United States and Canada," *The New England Journal of Medicine* 349 (2003): 768–775.

10. Centers for Medicare and Medicaid Services. Institute for Health Information, http://www.cms.hhs.gov/.

11. "Medicare data for calendar year 2003," Center for Medicare and Medicaid Services, http://www.cms.gov/.

12. "National Health Expenditures by Source of Funds 1999–2015," Centers for Medicare and Medicaid Services, http://www.cms.gov/.

13. "Understanding Health Plan Administrative Costs," Blue Cross and Blue Shield Association, http://www.bcbs.com/.

14. Centers for Medicare and Medicaid Services. Institute for Health Information, http://www.cms.hhs.gov/.

15. "Trends and Indicators in the Changing Health Care Marketplace," Kaiser Family Foundation, http://www.kff.org/.

16. "Annual Change in Health Insurance Premiums 1988–2005, Trendwatch Chartbook 2006," American Hospital Association, http://www.aha.org/.

Chapter 5

1. Centers for Medicare and Medicaid Services, http://www.cms.gov/.

2. Schoen, Cathy. "Insured But Not Protected: How Many Adults Are Underinsured?" *Health Affairs* (2005): Web Exclusive W5 289–302.

3. The Kaiser Commission on Medicaid and the Uninsured. "Recent Trends in Health Insurance Coverage, 2005," Kaiser Family Foundation, http://www.kff.org/.

4. Families USA Publication No. 05-101, June 2005. "Paying a Premium, The Added Cost of Care for the Uninsured," Families USA, http://www.familiesusa.org/.

5. Centers for Medicare and Medicaid Services, http://www.cms.gov/.

6. American Hospital Association, http://www.aha.org/.

7. Zuckerman, Stephen. "Changes In Medicaid Physician Fees, 1998–2003: Implications For Physician Participation," *Health Affairs* (2004): Web Exclusive W4 374–384.

8. Ibid.

9. The Kaiser Commission on Medicaid and the Uninsured. "Medicaid's High Cost Enrollees: How Much Do They Drive Program Spending?" Kaiser Family Foundation, http://www.kff.org/.

10. Ibid.

11. The Kaiser Commission on Medicaid and the Uninsured, May 2006. "Understanding the Recent Changes in Medicaid Spending and Enrollment Growth Between 2000–2004," Kaiser Family Foundation, http://www.kff.org/.

12. Levy, Robert. "The Cost Of Medicaid Annuities," *Health Affairs* 25 (2006): 444–451.

13. "Recent Trends in Health Insurance Coverage, 2005."

14. The Kaiser Commission on Medicaid and the Uninsured. "Figure 16, Nonelderly Uninsured by Family Work Status, 2004," Kaiser Family Foundation, http://www.kff.org/.

15. The Kaiser Commission on Medicaid and the Uninsured. "Who are the Uninsured—and Who Is at Risk?" Kaiser Family Foundation, http://www.kff.org/.

16. "Federal Poverty Level Charts, CMS, 2005," Centers for Medicare and Medicaid Services, http://www.cms.gov/.

17. "National Compensation Survey: Occupational Wages in the United States, July, 2004," U.S. Department of Labor, August 2005.

18. The Kaiser Commission on Medicaid and the Uninsured, 2005. "Figure 26, Uninsured Rates among Workers by Poverty Level and Firm Size, 2004," Kaiser Family Foundation, http://www.kff.org/.

19. Families USA, http://www.familiesusa.org/.

20. Health Research and Educational Trust. "Employer Health Benefits 2004 Annual Survey," Kaiser Family Foundation, http://www.kff.org/.

21. Families USA, http://www.familiesusa.org/.

22. Ibid.

23. Centers for Medicare and Medicaid Services, http://www.cms.gov/.

24. Families USA, http://www.familiesusa.org/.

25. Hadley, Jack. "How Much Medical Care Do the Uninsured Use, and Who Pays for It?" *Health Affairs* (2003): Web Exclusive W3 66–81.

26. "National Uncompensated Care Based on Cost: 1980–2004," November 2005, American Hospital Association, http://www.aha.org/.

27. Families USA, http://www.familiesusa.org/.

28. Hadley, "How Much Medical Care."

29. "Aggregate Hospital Payment-To-Cost Ratios For Private Payers, Medicare, and Medicaid 1981–2004, Trendwatch Chartbook 2006," American Hospital Association, http://www.aha.org/.

30. Families USA, http://www.familiesusa.org/.

31. Hadley, "How Much Medical Care."

32. Ibid.

33. "Health Care Cost Survey, August 2005," Kaiser Family Foundation, http://www.kff.org/.

34. Families USA, http://www.familiesusa.org/.

35. Hadley, "How Much Medical Care."

36. "Poverty in the United States," Wikipedia, http://www.wikipedia.org/ (accessed September 2, 2006).

37. Schoen, "Insured But Not Protected."

38. Ibid.

39. Ibid.

Chapter 6

1. "Innovation," PHRMA, Pharmaceutical Research and Manufacturers of America, 2006, http://www.phrma.org/.

2. "The Choice: Health Care for People or Drug Industry Profits," Families USA, http://www.familiesusa.org/.

3. "Trends and Indicators in the Changing Health Care Marketplace," Kaiser Family Foundation, http://www.kff.org/.

4. Ibid.

5. Families USA, http://www.familiesusa.org/.

6. U.S. Department of Commerce. "Pharmaceutical Price Controls in OECD Countries," International Trade Administration, http://www.ita.doc.gov/.

7. The European Association of Euro-Pharmaceutical Companies. "Benefits to Payers and Patients from Parallel Trade," York Health Economics Consortium, http://www.york.ac.uk/.

8. U.S. Department of Commerce.

9. The European Association of Euro-Pharmaceutical Companies.

10. Ibid.

11. Canadian Patented Drug Board Annual Report 2005. "Regulating Prices of Patented Medicines," Patented Medicine Prices Review Board, http://www.pmprb-cepmb.gc.ca/.

12. Pharmacy Checker, http://www.Pharmacychecker.com (accessed August 21, 2006).

13. U.S. Department of Commerce.

14. AARP Watchdog Report, April 2006. "Brand-Name Drug Prices Keep Going Up," AARP, http://www.AARP.org/.

15. "Prescription Drug Trends, June 2006," Kaiser Family Foundation, http://www.kff.org/.

16. Philbin, E. "Factors determining angiotensin-converting enzyme inhibitor underutilization in heart failure in a community setting," *Clinical Cardiology* 21 (1998): 103–108.

17. Sanal, S. "The effect of an educational program on the prevalence of use of antiplatelet drugs, beta blockers, angiotensin-converting enzyme inhibitors, lipid-lowering drugs, and calcium channel blockers prescribed during hospitalization and a hospital discharge in patients with coronary disease," *Journal of Gerontology Series A: Biological Sciences and Medical Sciences* 58 (2003): 1046–1048.

18. Gutierrez, M. "Underutilization of beta-adrenoceptor antagonists post-myocardial infarction," *American Journal of Cardiovascular Drugs* 1 (2005): 23–29.

19. Sackner-Bernstein, J. "Reducing the risks of sudden death and heart failure post myocardial infarction: utility of optimized pharmacotherapy," *Clinical Cardiology* 28, Supp. 1 (2005): 119–127.

20. Caro, J. "An economic model of stroke in atrial fibrillation: cost of suboptimal oral anticoagulation," *American Journal of Managed Care* 10, Supp. 14 (2004): 451–458.

21. Ghosh, S. "Underutilization of aspirin, beta blockers, angiotensin-converting enzyme inhibitors, and lipid-lowering drugs and overutilization of calcium channel blocker in older persons with coronary artery disease in an academic nursing home," *Journal of Gerontology Series A: Biological Sciences and Medical Sciences* 57 (2002): 398–400.

22. Sanal, "The effect of an educational program."

23. "Trends and Indicators in the Changing Health Care Marketplace."

Chapter 7

1. "Reform required to control liability premiums," *American Medical News*, November 21, 2005, Opinion Section.

2. Anderson, Gerard F. "Health Spending in the United States and the Rest of the Industrialized World," *Health Affairs* 24 (2005): 903–914.

3. Sorrel, Amy. "Failure to diagnose is the No. 1 allegation in liability lawsuits," *American Medical News,* March 20, 2006, Professional Issues Section.

4. Elmore, Joann. "Ten Year Risk of False Positive Screening Mammograms and Clinical Breast Examinations," *The New England Journal of Medicine* 338 (1998): 1089–1096.

5. "Defensive Medicine and Medical Malpractice," *Office of Technology Assessment, Congress of the United States, OTA H-602,* July 1994.

6. Studdert, David. "Defensive Medicine Among High-Risk Specialist Physicians in a Volatile Malpractice Environment," *JAMA* 293 (2005): 2609–2617.

7. Ibid.

8. Hillstead, Richard. "Can Electronic Medical Record Systems Transform Health Care? Potential Health Benefits, Savings, and Costs," *Health Affairs* 24 (2005): 1103–1117.

9. Anderson, Gerard F. "Health Care Spending and Use of Information Technology in OECD Countries," *Health Affairs* 25 (2006): 819–831.

10. Ibid.

11. Frisse, Mark. "State And Community-Based Efforts To Foster Interoperability," *Health Affairs* 24 (2005): 1190–1196.

12. "Trends and Indicators in the Changing Health Care Marketplace," Kaiser Family Foundation, http://www.kff.org/.

13. Berk, Marc. "The Concentration Of Health Care Expenditures, Revisited," *Health Affairs* 20 (2001): 9–18.

14. Bodenheimer, Thomas. "High and Rising Health Care Costs. Part 4: Can Costs Be Controlled While Preserving Quality?" *Annals of Internal Medicine* 143 (2005): 26–31.

15. Ibid.

16. Ibid.

17. Ibid.

18. Anderson, Gerard F. "Health Spending in the United States and the Rest of the Industrialized World," *Health Affairs* 24 (2005): 903-914.

19. Anderson, Gerard F. "It's the Prices, Stupid: Why the United States Is So Different from Other Countries," *Health Affairs* 22 (2003): 89–105.

20. Reinhardt, Uwe. "Cross-National Comparisons of Health Systems Using OECD Data, 1999," *Health Affairs* (2002): 169–181.

21. Organization for Economic Cooperation and Development, http://www.oecd.org.

22. Finkelstein, Eric. "State-Level Estimates of Annual Medical Expenditures Attributable to Obesity," *Obesity Research* 12 (2004): 18–24.

23. Simon, Paul. "Public Health And Business: A Partnership That Makes Cents," *Health Affairs* 25 (2006): 1029–1039.

24. Tobacco Information and Prevention Source. "Adult Cigarette Smoking in the United States: Current Estimates, Fact Sheet, December 2005," Centers for Disease Control and Prevention, http://www.cdc.gov/.

25. "The Impact of Smoking on Disease and the Benefits of Smoking Reduction," *The Health Consequences of Smoking,* Surgeon General's Report, 2004.

26. MMWR, July 1, 2005. "Annual Smoking-Attributable Mortality, Years Potential Life Lost, and Productivity Losses—United States, 1997–2001," Centers for Disease Control and Prevention, http://www.cdc.gov/.

27. Ibid.

28. MMWR, October 12, 2001. "Cigarette Smoking Among Adults—United States, 1999," Centers for Disease Control and Prevention, http://www.cdc.gov/.

29. MMWR, November 11, 2005. "Cigarette Smoking Among Adults—United States, 2004," Centers for Disease Control and Prevention, http://www.cdc.gov/.

30. Mark, Tami. "U.S. Spending for Mental Health and Substance Abuse Treatment, 1991–2001," *Health Affairs* (2005): Web Exclusive W5 133–142.

31. "Rate per 1,000 population of selected DSM-IV psychiatric disorders," National Institute on Alcohol Abuse and Alcoholism, http://www.niaa.nih.gov/.

32. Matano, Robert. "Prevalence of alcohol and drug use in a highly educated workforce," *Journal of Behavioral Health Services and Research* 29 (2002): 30–45.

Chapter 8

1. Brettenthaler, Reiner. "Comparison of the health care systems in the EU Member States," http://www.aerztekammer.at/service/EUSTUDPPT/98091.htm (accessed September 4, 2006).

2. Centers for Medicare and Medicaid Services. Institute for Health Information, http://www.cms.hhs.gov/.

3. Medicaid 2004 = $270 billion
Uninsured 2004 = $100 billion x 1.27 (increase from 2001)
Of the uninsured expenditures, out-of-pocket = 26%, uncompensated = 35%, public insurance = 14%, private insurance = 24%
2004 uncompensated care was $35 billion x 1.27 to get from 2001 to 2004

4. "National Health Expenditures by Source of Funds 1999–2015," Centers for Medicare and Medicaid Services, http://www.cms.gov/.

5. 2004 Canadian total expenditures $132 billion. 16.7% administrative expenses = $22 billion. 31.6 million people yields $696/person, which is $561 PPP U.S. 2004 Canadian total expenditures from Canadian Institute for Health Information (May 10, 2006).

6. Woolhandler, Steffie. "Costs of Health Care Administration in the United States and Canada," *The New England Journal of Medicine* 349 (2003): 768–775.

7. Ibid.

8. Ibid.

9. The Physicians' Working Group for Single-Payer National Health Insurance. "Proposal of the Physicians' Working Group for Single-Payer National Health Insurance," *JAMA* 290 (2003): 798–805.

10. "The World Health Report 2006," World Health Organization, http://www.WHO.org/.

11. Franks, P. "Health Insurance and Mortality. Evidence From A National Cohort," *JAMA* 270 (1993): 737–741.

12. Mc Williams, Michael. "Health Insurance Coverage and Mortality Among The Near-Elderly," *Health Affairs* 23 (2004): 223–233.

Epilogue

1. The Kaiser Commission on Medicaid and the Uninsured, May 10, 2002. " Sicker and Poorer: The Consequences of Being Uninsured," Kaiser Family Foundation, http://www.kff.org/.

2. Dranove, David. "Medical Bankruptcy: Myth Versus Fact," *Health Affairs* (2006): 74–83.

3. Himmelstein, David. "Illness and Injury as Contributions to Bankruptcy," *Health Affairs* (2005): Web Exclusive W5 63–73.

4. $1,400 from administration, $341 from private insurance, and $313 from Medicaid ($50 billion/160 million people—US population minus Medicaid, Medicare, and the uninsured)

5. "Socialized medicine," Dictionary.com, *Dictionary.com Unabridged (v 1.0.1)*, Random House, Inc., http://dictionary.reference.com/browse/socialized medicine (accessed December 2, 2006).

6. "Socialized medicine," Dictionary.com, *The American Heritage® Dictionary of the English Language, Fourth Edition*, Houghton Mifflin Company, 2004, http://dictionary.reference.com/browse/socialized medicine (accessed December 2, 2006).

7. "Socialized medicine," Dictionary.com, *The American Heritage® Stedman's Medical Dictionary.*, Houghton Mifflin Company, http://dictionary.reference.com/browse/socialized medicine (accessed December 2, 2006).

8. "Socialized medicine," Dictionary.com, *Merriam-Webster's Medical Dictionary*, Merriam-Webster, Inc., http://dictionary.reference.com/browse/socialized medicine (accessed December 2, 2006).

INDEX

Give the Gift of

U.S. Healthcare on Life Support
RESUSCITATING THE DYING SYSTEM
to Your Friends and Colleagues

CHECK YOUR LEADING BOOKSTORE OR ORDER HERE

❑ YES, I want _____ copies of *U.S. Healthcare on Life Support* at $15.95 each, plus $4.95 shipping per book (New Jersey residents please add $1.12 sales tax per book). Canadian orders must be accompanied by a postal money order in U.S. funds. Allow 15 days for delivery.

My check or money order for $_____ is enclosed.

Please charge my: ❑ Visa   ❑ MasterCard
                    ❑ American Express

Name_____

Organization _____

Address _____

City/State/Zip _____

Phone_____ Email _____

Card # _____   _____

Exp. Date_____ Signature _____

Please make your check payable and return to:
Denisher Press
PO Box 71, Haddonfield, NJ 08033-9998

Call your credit card order to: 856-795-0775
Fax: 856-795-6109   www.health-financing.com